FOX TALES

Selected Poetry
And Essays

Fox Tales

Selected Poetry
And Essays

James R. Fox

**The New
Atlantian Library**

THE NEW ATLANTIAN LIBRARY
is an imprint of
Absolutely Amazing eBooks

Published by Whiz Bang LLC, 926 Truman Avenue, Key West, Florida 33040, USA.

Fox Tales: Selected Poetry and Essays copyright © 2014 by Gee Whiz Entertainment LLC. Electronic compilation/ print edition copyright © 2014 by Whiz Bang LLC.

All rights reserved. No part of this book may be reproduced, scanned, or transmitted in any form or by any means, electronic or mechanical, including photocopying, recording, or any information storage and retrieval system, without permission in writing from the publisher. Please do not participate in or encourage piracy of copyrighted materials in violation of the author's rights. Purchase only authorized ebook editions.

This is an original work of poetry. Names, characters, places, and incidents either are the product of the author's imagination or are used fictitiously, and any resemblance to actual persons, living or dead, businesses, companies, events, or locales is entirely coincidental. While the author has made every effort to provide accurate information at the time of publication, neither the publisher nor the author assumes any responsibility for errors, or for changes that occur after publication. Further, the publisher does not have any control over and does not assume any responsibility for author or third-party websites or their contents.

For information contact:
Publisher@AbsolutelyAmazingEbooks.com

ISBN-13: 978-0692024157
ISBN-10: 0692024158

When inspired to write poetry or prose,
I place pen to paper
then commence to compose

FOX TALES

Selected Poetry
And Essays

Just Checkin' In:

If you are reading this, then my manuscript which I submitted was approved and has been published. I would greatly like to thank those who saw fit that what I have written was worthy enough to be printed. I shall forever be in your debt. To my family and friends I cannot express to you in words how much it means to me that your love support and understanding in regards to my writing has been inspiring and allows me to place pen to paper. And for those who I haven't met but by happenstance now have this book in your hands I thank you. So until I will be just checkin' in once more. Happy Trails to you 'til we meet again.

A Bedtime Story

Please tell me a bedtime story
I'm having trouble falling asleep
Please tell me a bedtime story
Then I promise I'll fall fast asleep
Do you want to hear about lions and tigers and bears?
Oh my, gosh no I've heard it so many times before
Read to me something original from the island far from shore
There once was a little boy and girl who were left all alone
On a small secluded island to fend for their own
Were animals there, or games that they could play?
If you keep on interrupting, I'll never have anything to say
There were zebras and to see them simply read between the lines
A family of leopards, connect the dots inside the vines
A group of penguins all marching in a row
There was even a pink elephant wearing a fancy bow
I see that your eyes are getting weary so I'll stop and tuck you in
Promise me before you leave, promise you'll come and visit me again
At the doorway of the child's room stood dear old mom and dad
Have you been talking again to your imaginary friend?

Fox Tales

We overheard everything you just said
Oh he isn't make believe, he's as real as you and I
But I have to keep him a secret I promised, crossed my heart and hope to die
So if you are a parent or better yet a child that lives inside your heart
There is a voice that stays with you forever
It is in the land of make believe from which you can never ever depart

A Cat's Whisker Away From the Hair of a Dog

Day old stale bread crumbs beats being hungry
If you're one of the many who lives out on the street
I'll tell you no lie, scotch, bourbon, whiskey and rye
Will take from you more than the liver and teeth
Oh where are you going my daughter my son?
All dressed up, stay don't go, let's have some fun
Far too many days, I've been all alone, wanting to see your face
My how you've grown now on your own a new job in a new place
There once was a time when I was doing fine had it all it came so fast
But I wanted more, thought I knew the score, but it didn't last
A turn of events, lost it all, flat broke, I was a total mess
I sank to the bottom of a bottle, guzzling at full throttle no time to confess
We all have our ups and downs
Our demons, angels, jugglers, clowns
That is what makes us our DNA from our fingerprints down to our soles
It doesn't mean a bag of beans the rich in rags, the beggar in fancy clothes

Fox Tales

Not only does a dwelling need an annual spring cleaning
One must get rid of the cobwebs in our lives if you get my
   meaning

A Cup of Coffee and a Piece of Pie

It seems to me these days that everyone has an opinion, can't agree on who is to blame for the mess we're in. Those in the know all belong to the millionaires club bask in the spotlight and tell us how they are going to solve the problems, if you just vote for them.

Well, that is the trouble, me or you can't be heard, much less seen because we're worried about making ends meet, will we be able to pay the bills, put food on the table and have spare change at the end of the week to put into the poor box after saying our respects to the Lord.

I lead a simple life, give me a flannel shirt, pair of jeans, comfortable shoes and I'm good to go. I don't need a fancy car or expensive gifts to make me happy. I'd rather read a book, listen to what a friend has to say enjoy music or quiet solitude.

Some might think that if you're not expressing how you feel by texting or social networking you're out of the loop, well then that's where I want to be. I don't need to ask how is the weather I only have to look out the window or step outside, easy as that.

I don't need a panel of experts to draw maps, fancy words or phrases to tell me how we arrived in dire straits and when it will eventually get better. There have been times before when the ground underfoot was shaky, the downtrodden on breadlines, wars, the unemployed, despair and somehow the country didn't shatter and disappear.

Back then there was leadership everyone pulled together, a sense of pride not self-pity. A house divided cannot stand a great man once said that and the message cannot be more prevalent than the times we are living in. Instead of focusing on the stock market, reality shows, the absurdity of the rich and famous, take care of what matters most. What or who can you help or who can help you?

Seldom there are second chances, or do over's or getting out of jail cards. It all comes down to ABC'S on blocks of wood that helped us grow up. I've got a tunnel full of questions but a hobo's chance of solving them or making it to the end of the line before getting kicked off because maybe that's the way it's supposed to be.

Why do bad things happen to good people and yet others get away with murder and unimaginable acts of depravity? Walk a mile with a strangers crutches, propel a wheelchair over obstacles, the blind may not see but can hear the deaf may not hear but can see. There but for the grace of God go I.

You can't lasso a calf without a rope, you can't fight a bull without a cape, you can't catch a fish without some bait, it can't be black if its white, can't be day if its night and it can't be wrong if it's right.

A Thimble, a Needle & Thread

There is a four-poster bed and an old rocking chair
Where I sat beside grandma Grace, as I brushed her silver hair
She had just celebrated her birthday, of one hundred years a century
On the left hand she wore a wedding band, an expression of her fidelity
As I watched where she lay, she smiled and said to me
It was on a hot summer day, back in thirty-three
I was on my way to church in my fancy dress
When an auto pulled up driven by a handsome lad I must confess
He honked the horn as he sat inside a shiny black Tin Lizzy
I was startled and his looks made me feel dizzy
Why hi there pretty lady, what's your name he said to me
Never you mind I replied I've somewhere to go, can't you see?
Can I take you for a drive, to the matinee picture show?
I promise to be a gentleman, why I'll even drive slow
He looked so dashing in that straw hat and fancy tie
My heart was all a flutter, I do declare, I thought I'd die
C'mon what do you say, let me take you for a ride
How do I know you don't holdup banks like Bonnie & Clyde?

Fox Tales

What was I to do my legs had suddenly turned into lead
He idled the motor, stepped out and said his name was Fred
I was speechless as I sheepishly replied I'm Grace
Well that makes sense said he, for you have such a pretty face
Well we courted for a spell, until one day decided to wed
We were both dirt poor, but saved up for this four poster bed
Then grandma's eyes slowly closed as she drifted off to sleep
I sat there in the darkness, trying not to make a peep
But it was only for a moment, when her eyes opened then lifted her head
Is that you Fred, why are you here, don't you realize you are dead?
I remember, for I'll never forget, it was in the winter of forty-four
When you were sent overseas, to fight in that God awful war
Then came the day I received a letter,
That was a kin to an outbreak of smallpox
Taps were played, the children and I at the cemetery
Wept over your pine coffin box
I don't know how I survived, oh the rivers that I cried
As I looked at our wedding album, I could not accept my true love had died
I raised the family on my own, sewed their clothes
With a thimble, a needle and thread
Then before shutting off the light, read a passage
From the good book before going to bed

James R. Fox

These were her last dying words as a smile crossed her face
Now at last in heaven, with grandpa Fred, my amazing grandma Grace

Rumbling, Rambling and Gambling

The rumbling rambling and gambling
In this world of handling
Gems from the Far East
Peasants present at the feast
Fiery torches surround the tents
Windswept ruins reveal little semblance
Of what was, a forbidden dynasty
A journey of uncertain odyssey
Here in the labyrinth of apothecary mazes
A wizard concocts a potion in phases
Hazel root warthog ears of every ones fears
Jangling of keys as the blind monk nears
Castle on a hill in a fog at night
Chessboard is missing a bishop of white
Uncertainty the quest of the prophet that a waits
Passes judgment on all the sinners as well as the saints
Tealeaves are read to solve a mystery
A glimpse into hidden personal history
Shades that hide the map, the manuscript, the sacred book
Are behind closed doors where curious eyes can never look

Afternoon Muse

Couplets sonnets and words that often rhyme
Are in syncopation as the shadows
Cast on the sundial mark the time
Only the weary tire from the walk
Only the winded tire from the talk
The mistress of the seas
Becomes the hunted when the waters are calm
But she knows only too well
When to cast the spell
Oh ye of little faith
The hour is near
Take match to wick
Keep loved ones near
Place pen to paper
Lyrics in line
Fill up the chalice
With the Lords finest wine

FAMILY

What creates a connection and others not
What creates a bow and some a knot
What ties people together
While others tend to forget
Where memories stand the test of time
When loved ones are gone forever
The steps that are taken
The shadows that set in
The webs that are spun
The hardships which accompany the triumphs
Chances tossed which are seldom won
For what is it that defines a family?
Aunts and uncles cousins, nieces and nephews
To have goodness in our souls
We need every one of these pieces

DAUGHTERS

Three angels came into our lives
Spaced between a few years apart
One angel was quiet, another full of joy
And the other more than once broke our heart
We did our best in the early years
Protected and wiped away their tears
Watched them grow from little girls
Of Cabbage Patch dolls and pretty curls
How fast those days swept by
Tuck me in tell me a story
Cross my heart and hope to die
Good night mom and dad
Turn off the lights and do not cry
They made such pretty brides
On their wedding day
We were so proud of them
No longer little girls
It seems like just yesterday
Today our home is quiet
All the toys are put away
Their dolls are in the attic
We'll take them they promise
But not right now, not today
I have many memories of my angels
They are stored and locked away
Forever to remain my treasure

Fox Tales

Daughters and their fathers
Are special that way

God Is In The Garden

God is in the garden
Watching the flowers bloom
He cultivates and waters
Creating life within the womb
He sprinkles each and every one
Lists them all and gives them life
You see His garden is filled with babies
Some will be healthy, others will have strife
A baby is a special gift
That comes from heaven above
It is our responsibility
To see they grow with love
God plants many crops
Watches each and every one
We come in many colors
The Lords work is never done
So if you have time to give
A child could use some love
For we are what we sow
God is watching from above

You Always Complete Me

Your gentle voice becomes notes to a melody
Your eyes are the colors used to paint a portrait
You are there to lift me when I am down
You never shun or ignore
You always complete me

Whatever I need you gladly give
When friends are hard to come by
You are never too busy or preoccupied
If I may trip stumble or fall
Who is there to answer the call?
You always complete me

Times in the year change with the seasons
And so it goes for those we cherish
We fall in love, marry raise a family
The children grow and follow their dreams
A quiet home contains fleeting memories
More is less, as less is more
You always complete me

My dreams are a patch quilt
Woven and spun by a spider
My ship has no compass
Nor a navigational chart

Fox Tales

But if my dreams never come true
And my vessel is lost in a storm
It would have been all worth knowing that
You always complete me

Platitude and Gratitude

Platitude and Gratitude
Are wearisome companions
Riding in a Corvette coupe
Heading out for the canyons

Fuzzy dice hanging on the rearview mirror
Made from exotic imported foam
Buffing up the toes of my boots
Leaning on the gleaming chrome

Long sleeve shirt buttoned at the cuffs
Sunglasses hiding bloodshot eyes
Silver tipped laces sparkle
From evenly hung bolo ties

Faded jeans torn at the knees
Wheels a spinning kicking up dirt
Belt buckle inscribed
With initials double B's

Radio playing a country tune
Buckboard up ahead being pulled by a mule
Down shifting gears knuckles turning white
Crossing over solid line acting like a fool

Fox Tales

Eighteen-wheeler moving way too fast
Reason to believe already it's way too late
Made tomorrows paper front-page photo and wait
In bold headlines a date with fate
SHOULD HAVE TAKEN THE INTERSTATE

Unfolding a Dream

How easy it would be to say what I mean
To put into words and escape from the dream
As shadows develop from the corners of the room
Eclipse the sun from the approaching moon

Thoughts are sincere a novel notion
The sorcerer conjures up the deadly potion
The lady in waiting sits and listens
To the troubadours melody that glistens

The cold winds of November
Beckon me to remember
Once when I was so much younger
Fleeting moments that I hunger

Forever gone are those that I cherish so well
Whom I wish to say come back just for a spell
We are here at a particular season
Selection has no definition or reason

Hands that used to be so agile
Now are arthritic wrinkled and vile
It has vanished never to be seen
Mirrors the image but never the dream

The Poet is in the Alley

Bob Dylan is indeed the poet in the alley
Strumming his guitar tellin' us his views
Recitin' the news
Enfolding melodies
Like a velvety draped muse

He is the rhymer of reason
A year of four seasons
And takes the time to explain
Examine the facts retrace the steps
Amid the deluge
Of loss and of pain

A wayward minstrel
That wants everyone to hear
Come listen to the message
From a once younger
Now so much older balladeer

Some carry a lot of trouble
Down the road of rust and rubble
Others wake at the break of noon
As for me, well I'll just keep on a listenin'
Showin' less expression
But always a whistlin'
One of my favorite Dylan tunes

A Single Note of a Trumpet

A single note of a trumpet
Can be heard at midnight
While little boy lost
Searches for his kite
The old lady she knows where it's at
She took it and hid it
But he'll never guess that
Ah Suzy, she's so cute
With her dimple cheeks, curly hair
And a radiant suit
The crippled man and dragon slayer
Crawl up and down the street
Trying to get at the mayor
Who they are dying to meet
He's in the parlor, concealed in a concrete slab
And all his assassins outside
Won't ever get in
To make their deadly stab
The beggar and the fool cannot approach
For they live on sewer filled streets
While the queen she rides in a coach
The bricks they lay so carefully
As if by some plan
While the hungry go unfed
Searching in an empty garbage can

Fox Tales

The addict in the alley he really needs a fix
While the mayor's son
Drops acid and LSD for his kicks
The peasants die in numbers
But who does it hurt
For the royalty the bourgeois
Consider everyone dirt
Storm the gates the people cry
Come on lets scale the walls
We'll take the life of the king and queen
And let their blood flow in the halls
And so they did ten thousand strong
With stones and bricks and bows
Even though they knew
What they were doing was wrong
They captured the castle
And slew everyone in sight
And now a single note of a trumpet
Can be heard at midnight
For the peasants now the bourgeois
Really lost the fight

Telling about Life

In these times of toil and tribulation
People judge guilty the younger generation
They put them down for the way they act
And say we never ever did that
They say that the music and long hair must go
But can't look back in history not long ago
When they did things that weren't so good
While now we do them also but we're called hoods
Ask me what I feel about this world
Where a dying bird just lies on the ground
Where rains are always tumbling down
Where people walk around with no faces
To many undetermined outlandish places
Where sin is the winner
And being good is for squares
Where children have no future to look to
Because of what our leaders will promise they will do
If you were a hermit you would live fine
But I'd never let you enter this world of mine
Where people are starving by the number
But no one seems to care about the other
Your fellow man could die in front of your face
But you would never stop
For fear of stepping out of pace
Right now a bird sings a song for someone
Right now a man cries over a lost one

Fox Tales

Right now a baby dies for lack of food
Right now a lion is having a zebra for dinner
Right now one is drowning for he is not a swimmer
Right now the world's chances of surviving are getting slimmer
Turn your ears away and say I am not a speaker
Turn your mind away and say I am not a thinker
Walk away and say I'm a beginner
Tell me I have to grow
Into a man of tomorrow from a boy of long ago
Who decides who shall live or who shall die?
Who shall laugh and who shall cry?
Who shall be loved and who'll not be loved?
Whose dreams will come true?
Or whose life will be a train
Whose destination is only one place isolation?
Who makes the rules in this game known as life?
Where each day is a struggle of strife
You tell me all you learned men
Tell me over and over again
Then go hide under your rock
Until someone like me
Searches for answers
And begins to knock

O Where Have You Been My Blue Eyed Son?

He wore James Dean's coat of red
A scarf around his neck
Drove his motorcycle down the road
Then took lay lady lay to bed

He went knockin' on heaven's door
Became tangled up in blue
Stayed for a spell at the Chelsea Hotel
We called him a genius others labeled him a boor

The times they are a changin'
Look around these words hold true
Wars rivers a ragin'
Sang sad eyed lady of the lowlands for me and you

Today they say he is out of time
All washed up past his prime
Lost his rhythm got too old
Might even consider him fool's gold

Somewhere a spotlight will shine on the stage
Somewhere a singer will play his tunes
Someday they will discover amazing things
Dylan's work buried beneath the dunes

HARLEQUIN

My old guitar I can't play no more
It's missing a couple of strings
The rain outside is fallin' down
Birds can't fly on wet wings

Met a couple of angels
Just the other day
In the house of the Lord
We knelt and began to pray

Saw the boats later that night
The sky was painted with pastels of light
Cow bells fastened with frayed cord
Faded billboards posting room and board

Hopscotch butterscotch whiskey and rye
Tell us a bedtime story
We cross our hearts
And promise not to cry

Tomcats in the alley
Walking atop a rickety fence
Neighbors playin' a game of solitaire
Missin' the one eyed jack makes no sense

Forget Wishes Granted by a Genie

Thank you Lord for this day
For my many blessings
Is there anything I can do for thee?
Perhaps a task, a chore undone
What will ye have of me?

What is that you say my Lord?
I just cannot hear your voice
For you are so far away
Am I to make a choice?

If I possessed a magic lamp
That dwelled inside a genie
And would grant me three wishes
I wouldn't ask for wealth or health
Or a world full of riches

I would ask to see you
Face to face my Lord
That would be my first
I would save the others
Keep them in a safe place

I wish I were a painter
Who could create, a masterpiece

Fox Tales

Or a composer of music
Maestro conduct pretty please

Yes my Lord I understand
Be happy for what I have
The ability to comprehend
What less fortunate souls lack

Icicles melt on the eaves
Mittens warming by the stove
Do children really know?
What Santa has in his sack

I have so many words
To say to you my Lord
Occupy rooms in my head
Keep me up late at night
Dancing in concentric circles
Daylight is for thinking
Nighttime is for bed

I admired Hemingway
For writing where he stood
Poe, Michelangelo, Steinbeck, Rockwell too
Were so prolific
Just by your loving grace
Always encouraging so they could

What is that you say my Lord?
Say once more so that I can hear
Whisper sweet words so swiftly

James R. Fox

As lovers Sir Lancelot to Lady Guinevere

Are there any final requests
Is there anything I can do for you?
Yes be humble my poetaster
Always do what you enjoy
And always enjoy what you do

Dreams of mine even wishes
I know might never come true
But for this one thing I know for certain
That whenever you pray
God listens He always has the time
Not some wizard behind a colored curtain

October Rain

Rain, raindrops like a beating drum
Fast hands always a blur
Pirates, shipwrecks, cases of rum
Hearing messages unable to concur

Passports fingerprints documentations
Final destination no timetable for lamentations
On the road without advice
Do, it once better do it twice

Sit by the fire, sit for a spell
Light up your pipe, sip some freshly brewed tea
I have some interesting news to tell
I know your secrets only too well

A coven of witches black cats and such
May bother a closed mind
Does not matter to me so much
Because true believers are always blind

WAITING

Tapping ones fingers to the music of the past
Shadows of friends that would go and come
Like a freight train of box cars
And one lonesome caboose
Please don't take my covers
I need them more than ever
Lost is this shell of a man
On a beach of despair
Footprints push aside the grains
Allow the incoming tide
To wash it all away
One too many afternoons
Alone with just a heartbeat
That keeps me company
Proper planning is an ingredient
Vital in the diet of life
Know what is attainable
As well as available
Ponder yonder
Set your sails
Trusting that fair trade winds
Will steer your course
Navigate with your dreams among the stars
Take your position
Let your emotions propel you
To that place

Fox Tales

*You have always
Wanted to go
Time has a funny way
Of creeping up on you
One day we are playing stickball
Doing homework going to the movies
Then we are walking down the aisle
Having children, being parents
Then becoming grandparents
Aches and pains suddenly appear
That you never had before
I cannot remember being
On this highway
How did I get here?
How the hell
Do I return to being me?*

TAPS

From the halls of Montezuma to the shores of Tripoli
On the deck of the U.S.S. Constitution
I have defended our countries freedom
Bugler play Taps for me

At Bunker Hill they stood their ground
For all the Redcoats to see
The Minutemen fired their muskets
Bugler plays Taps for me

Paul Revere rode so gallantly
Alerting the citizens that night
One if by land two if by sea
Bugler play Taps for me

As brother-to-brother we fought each other
A nation torn asunder
Some followed Grant as well as Robert E. Lee
Bugler play Taps for me

We fought in the trenches in the First World War
Against our bitter foe Germany
Some of us returned home, while others not
Bugler play Taps for me

Fox Tales

On a beautiful Sunday morning in the harbor at Pearl
Came suicide squadrons of Imperial Japan Zeros
Our sailors and soldiers fought and died bravely
Bugler play Taps for me

We stormed the beaches at Normandy
Withstood the Nazi Panzer tanks
Liberated Europe from the deadly grip of tyranny
Bugler play Taps for me

In a far off land divided in two
We held our ground at Pork Chop Hill
Now only a forgotten long lost memory
Bugler play Taps for me

In paddies of rice they seemed so nice
Placed our POW'S inside the Hanoi Hilton
Tortured and paraded our heroes for all of the world to see
Bugler play Taps for me

On nine eleven in the year two thousand and one
Terrorists from a distant Middle East Arab land
Rained fire and brimstone as if it were a Biblical prophesy
Bugler play Taps for me

And so it began and so it shall continue
From once a tiny acorn that took root
Now a mighty oak truly a majestic Tree of Liberty
Bugler play Taps for me

James R. Fox

There are many who have passed
In graveyards they peacefully lie
My brothers in arms who I cannot see
Bugler play Taps for me

Memorial Day

To those of us that are assembled here today, it is a day of perhaps overtime if need be. To others, it is the first weekend to open your pool in the backyard. Tend to the kids kick back with family and friends. Who wants cheese on their burgers? Love those Knicks!

How about the Yanks and the Mets? Do you think they'll have another Subway Series?

Memorial Day: Battlefields

Concord and Lexington, the Alamo, Gettysburg, the Little Big Horn, Sand Juan Hill, Belleau Wood, Pearl Harbor, Normandy Beach, Pork Chop Hill.

We have fought on many lands: Europe, Korea, Vietnam, the Middle East. Lost soldiers and sailors their eyes wide open frozen in time fought to keep and preserve freedom for the rest of us.

Old Glory a piece of cloth the colors red white and blue withstood the British cannons that inspired Francis Scott Key to write The Star Spangled Banner, long may she wave. Atop Mount Surabachi on Iwo Jima a group of Marines raised our flag for all to see.

For all of us that are present, consider the following the next time you see our flag. Imagine if you can the white stripes signify hope. The blue stripes pure freedom, as eagles soar high above in an azure sky. The red stripes denote all of the blood that has been shed for this country so that all of us and our future generations shall live in peace and freedom.

May we always respect and pray for our brave and heroic veterans and remember the forgotten POW'S and those among us who are homeless and in need of assistance. May God bless America the greatest country on Earth and to all the veterans I proudly salute each and every one.

A Beacon of Hope

From the very first time our eyes met
I felt a presence in the air
Was it the rain so cold so wet?
Or the scent of your lustrous flaxen hair

The carnival horses of the carousel
The festive music that which we heard
The gloves you wore the parasol
We spoke in silence without a word

We made love in the lighthouse
Our shadows on the wall entwined
Quietly as a pair of church mice
You suddenly disappeared I shall never find

So now I seek you out at sea
For I have lost and can never be
Searching my soul losing my sanity
You call you call out for me

Winter's Chill

All the papers and pages that I carry
Contain the solace of tomorrow if I tarry
In the order of importance I was given
To deliver the correspondence I was driven
To perchance a curiosity I developed
To an attractive widow I enveloped
I shan't mention her name
For my heart is a flame
Precisely kept my reputation to remember
In the wintry winds of December
Windows frosted over, trimming of the tree
Fond memories they shall forever be
Blankets of white on a Christmas Eve night
Have children dreaming of fun and delight
Bright packages with ribbon and seal
Contain gifts which cost a great deal
As the candle flickers its last light
Window shutters are drawn hidden from sight
Morning shall bring another new day
Will bring news from faraway
Messages in letters, words and rhyme
Postman be prompt be exactly on time

The Legend of Lefty

While the radio plays various familiar tunes
Grandson Kyle enjoys games and watches cartoons
My mind tends to pause and wander
Back to the Old West and yonder
West of the Pecos, and South of the Rio Grande
There once lived the fiercest hombre to lead a band
Of desperados behind bandanas, who robbed banks and shared the loot
As the posse hot on their trail didn't hesitate to shoot
Just mention the name El Diablo could lose your life
Say a prayer for the dearly departed Pablo, left a family and a wife
With a scar from a knife, El Diablo always dressed in black
Robbed Texas banks told the tellers put the money into the sack
Away he would ride atop his palomino across the divide
To the Mexican hideout in a cantina, aptly called suicide
Then came the time just about dawn
A day both sides will forever mourn
While the desperados were sleeping
From a night of hard drinking
A red rooster strutted across the road commenced to crowing
A cloud of dust followed a posse into town knowing
Little Jose he was the first to see
The badge of the Marshal named Jubal Lee
Inside the cantina, Juan the blind guitarist started to

strum
Nodded along as he whistled a tune continued to hum
El Diablo thumbs his sombrero above a pair of dark Latin eyes
Kicks over a chair, raises two pistols and cries
Today is the day that may be our last fight
Impossible senor, exclaims the bartender for we are out of sight
Meanwhile the posse, ride tall down along the rutted and grooved main street
Dismount from their saddles, tie up the horses, feel the morning suns heat
Marshal Lee leads them up the steps, carrying a double barrel shotgun
You are surrounded give up peacefully there is no place to run
El Diablo smiles a devilish grin, strikes a match lights a cigar
Buenos Dias gringo, have a shot of tequila with me at the bar
Mano to mano, face to face all await
Only the swinging doors separate their fate
What makes you think that our day is done?
The Federale's, the army with cannons they have come
Yet here I stand before you gringo, brave and still in command
Slowly and steady pistols are pulled by posse and the band
Fingers cock the hair triggers of silver handle Colt .44's
I'll give you a minute not one second more
Come out with your hands held high holding your holster strap

James R. Fox

You think I am but a fool to step into your trap?
If we come out it will be with guns a blazing
Then gringo, you and your posse will see something truly amazing
It was impossible to figure
Who, pulled the quicker trigger
Splinters of wood were all that were left of the cantinas door
Bottles of whiskey, shattered shot glasses, bodies fell to the floor
When the gun smoke cleared all was silent, except for the crunch
Of hob nailed boots, silver spurs spinning, the freshly dead bunch
Somewhere in the sunset a cowboy rides out for the range
Someplace where the cactus and the mesquite are not so strange
It is where a young widow wears a tattered gingham gown
It is where a senorita hides behind a serape tears falling down
The campfire casts shadows of two figures on the box canyon wall
They face each other once more, one shall win, one shall fall
Legends live forever inside the hearts of men
Told to the young ones time and again

Letters Received Letters Not Written

I have letters that await the postal station
Explaining my deepest regards of the fondest situation
When words that are meant to be spoken
Never are stated are left behind and broken
Family and seldom an occasional friend
Down the road or up the bend
The music flows from the next room
Like the flowers just waiting to bloom
A blue faded denim shirt hangs on the door
It is wrinkled and old could possibly clothe the poor
What is important to me, that are right
Words I need to hear and to write
Poets who are fluent can always create
Illusions for serendipitous pedestrians outside the gate
We are who we are it is as basic as that
Abstract art, scuba diving, a favorite movie, a Maine coon cat
A circle of friends are drawn for protection
Not for criticism amusement and never for inspection

Sleight of Hand

As I traveled along a rural and unfamiliar back road
I pulled into a gas station where I was told
I have gone a long way for being lost
Stay for the night and rest with very little cost
At the Twin Forks Inn across from the lake
Miss Sally may be old but man can she bake
Thanks for the directions plus the suggestion maybe I will
I proceeded out of town, passed an old gristmill
It was almost sundown as the sky grew dark
I was distracted by a shadow in the park
The figure resembled a gent dressed in strange clothes
Sporting a tall hat, white gloves, pince-nez spectacles perched on his nose
In his left hand was an ornate silver walking stick
Suddenly a cold chill ran up my back I began to feel sick
For whatever the reason as if possessed I had no clue
I mysteriously arrived at the Twin Forks Inn as if on cue
Behind the front desk sat a kindly old gent
Good evening I inquired do you have a room to rent?
Just for tonight then I'll be on my way
Take room number 3 it's at the end of the hall
Breakfast at 7 sharp I'll give you a call
I unlocked the door to the room with a brass skeleton key
But once inside I felt an eerie presence very close to me
I clicked on the old brass lamp just beside the bed
Turned down the covers to remove my fear and dread

Fox Tales

It couldn't have been but merely a few minutes hence
Outside the window I glanced at a rusty fence
A figure all in black advanced into the light
I was frozen in the bed mesmerized at the sight
A deck of cards from inside a vest jacket pocket
Swift hands held them along with a golden locket
The cards were fanned out to erase any doubt
In my mind what the stranger was all about
He said not a word only the sound of the cards could be heard
As he shuffled them they sounded like wings of a bird
I awoke early the next morning
From a deep sleep for I was snoring
I have never felt so rested and so serene
Can I surmise or was it all but a dream?
It was weeks later as I read in the paper while I sat in the back yard
An estate sale of a rustic old inn consisting of clothes, a locket and a card
As I continued to read there was a knock at the front door
I folded the paper to return to it later curious to know more
I opened the door and was handed a letter addressed to me
By a uniformed courier the letter simply stated RFD
I opened the seal wondering what could possibly be inside
With no return address who would want to hide?
A single piece of paper folded in two that held a worn playing card
Not a jack, king or queen but the figure which stood in the yard

James R. Fox

His sleeves were rolled up arms in plain view
The purpose I guess was to impress for only he knew
Never to have been seen before until then
To this very day I still remember when
Watching magic in the middle of the night
A sleight of hand much to my delight

What's in a Name?

Xylophones, saxophones tubas and bassoons

Oboes, harps cymbals and Saturday cartoons

Fifes, piccolos flutes melodious notes

Standup bass, playing third base, counting all the votes

Electric guitar, be who you are, be brave and follow your star

Microphone, lonesome at home, last call at the bar

Accordion playing sea shanty jigs, American Pie falls out of the sky

Jazz and blues, worrisome news, whose name I wonder why

All Roads Lead to Gettysburg

It was early in July when the air was hot and dry
History was about to be made where many would die
That the battle lines were slowly being drawn
Like pieces on a chessboard each man as if a pawn
General Lee and his Rebel forces were advancing toward town
General Meade's Union army were bracing for what was about to go down
On farmer's fields both sides refused to yield
A badge of honor, tattered regimental banners would be their only shield
There wasn't time to run, nor a place to hide
The Blue and Gray continued to advance far and wide
Through the Wheatfield, Peach Orchid and the Cemetery
Shots were fired prayers were said inside the Seminary
Be brave, yield no ground, now is not the time to retreat
It is here on this land stand fast we shall not be beat
The battle raged on for three continuous days
At Devil's Den, the Railroad Cut, the Baltimore Pike clouded in a haze
Volley after volley the cannons did roar increasingly louder
Rations of food, medical supplies running low, but not the gunpowder
Both sides battling through the shrouded dense fog of war

Fox Tales

At Plum Run, Culp's Hill, Big & Little Round Top
Both sides intent to even the score
The Southern States opted to throw down the gauntlet by
    voting to secede
That became the Crimson Tide the moon was high
An opportune time to recede
Adrift and far away from the beaches of inclusion justice
    and equality
The black slaves in chains prayed to the Lord above set
    your people free
Side by side in colors of Blue and Gray they fought,
Many wounded many more died
Thousands upon thousands double quick upon the
    furrowed fields of suicide
On the 4th of July General Lee assessed all that was lost
Some would live to tell others fell to defend at such a
    deadly cost
Honest Abe visited Gettysburg a few months later
In the middle of November
To consecrate these hallowed grounds
So future generations shall always remember
That in the course of human events no greater love can
    there be
Than to lay down one's life for your fellow man in defense
    of our liberty

To Be Adored

The animals were there first to bear witness
Of the sacred birth to the baby Jesus
There was stillness in the night
Stars were the beacons that showed the way
For the Magi who traveled from far away
Mother Mary held him much to her delight
Joseph knelt keeping the flock in his sight
We hold the birth of Jesus in our hearts
Pilgrims are weary come from many parts
To listen to the story from so long ago
Children sing Christmas carols so all will know
Our Savior came from heaven as a child
To heal the sick, raise the dead, calm the wild
Taught in the temples for the scholars to see
For this he was ridiculed, accused of preaching blasphemy
Jesus for a spell worked as a carpenter, making objects out of wood
Performed miracles of loaves and fish, water into wine because he could
Twelve were chosen to be the fishers of men
Had no idea where their faith would lead them
Peter denied Our Lord proclaiming he did not know him
Judas sold his soul ended his life hanging from a tree limb
The Christ was arrested taken to Pontius Pilate
Mother Mary heard the news a little too late
The Prince of Peace was to wear a crown of thorns

Fox Tales

Tortured by the Romans the faces of the crowd all with scorn
He carried a cross upon his bloody whipped back
To the hill of Calvary the sky drew dark and black
Nails in his arms and crossed feet
Two thieves on either side he would greet
Jesus looked to the heavens in agony as he hung
Forgive them Father for they know not what they have done
The earth shook it rained with heavens tears
Mother Mary's heart broke from her worst fears
Her son was wrapped in a simple death shroud
Placed inside a tomb an angel watched from a cloud
Jesus descended into hell for only a spell
To redeem the lost souls, to purify, to make them well
He reigns in heaven along with Our Father
Where the Holy Spirit and all the angels gather
Mother Mary in radiance the bluest of blue
All of my prayers I say today, I say them to you

A Kaleidoscope in a Snow Globe

When the last word ever spoken has been said
And when the last hungry child has been fed
Bitterest of enemies have fired their last gun
And peace shall finally come to every one
Where colors shall sit and feast at the table
And the lion and lamb will share the stable
The blind will lead the blind to the river
Where they will be baptized by truth and deliver
When promises are said and never ever broken
Wedding vows and rings exchanged as a token
On the last day of life as death will come
To gather the many and tally the sum
Where few are in number but matter just the same
Like wilted desert flowers that need fresh drops of rain
It is so easy to turn your back
To step aside and deny what others lack
For are we not our brother's keeper
Contained in our souls only so much deeper
So if we are granted a place and time
That allows us the chance to express and rhyme
All of us to live in a world without any fear
Of open hearts gladly with family and friends ever so near

Baby Steps

Baby steps are the hardest to take
Because we fear what is at stake
Do we rather just call it a day?
Turn our backs and walk away
How easy it would be to sit pat
Ignore and bore each other playing tit for tat
A new year approaches with hope and promise
Hear the news abandon a doubting Thomas
It is so much easier to shut the mind
Leave all your cares loves and family far behind
But someday after all the makeup cannot cover the glory
When only forgotten memories stored away are a long ago story
Now they are torn and hang as if a weathered worn awning
It shall be a little too late for tears at the mourning

DELUGE

Why are we still standing here with muskets at the ready?
Can't you plainly see that the levee is too unsteady?
And it soon came to pass and none too soon
Lake Ponchatrain and the Ole Miss came together
As if a tsunami, a South Seas typhoon
Hurricane Katrina came a blowin'
Shook the very foundation
All animals and folks a knowin'
With not a boat to row
Nor a road to go
Who will be left to save?
When all will be swept away to a watery grave
As the nation watched the turbulent waters rise
All left adrift and stranded before our very eyes
A funeral parade kept tempo
For a once long last look
Waterlogged photos, torn out pages
Of a family's life, a sacred holy book
Tambourines, tubas even a big bass drum
Tears, bourbon, Mardi-Gras beads
Crushed and lost amid the confusion and fun
The hurricane brought forth a flood
Of Biblical proportions
The poor lost all their possessions
The rich lost all their fortunes
For many days from Biloxi to the Big Easy

Fox Tales

The polluted waters, the air of uncertainty
Left everyone a little bit queasy
We take from the land turn our backs to the sea
Refuse to accept what eventually shall be
That when you don't plan for tomorrow
And waste what we have today
Then Mother Nature will soon come a callin'
To take everything she gave and washes it all away

The Frozen River

In the middle of winter on a jet black night
I tossed off my covers and turned on the light
For whatever the reason I really don't know
But I soon was all dressed outside in the snow
The street was deserted at this hour of day
I began a brisk pace, the cold wind in my face
It began snowing the flakes froze my ruddy cheeks
From the look of things, a thaw will take weeks
As I crossed the bridge to the other bank I started to think
When I was younger I skated on the river as if it were a rink
Played hockey with the gang hadn't the faintest clue
Joined the Navy right after Pearl Harbor, still carry an anchor tattoo
My beard that once was red is now many shades of gray
The world is out of focus, or maybe I'm just in the way
I turn up the collar of my old worn pea coat
Spot an old sea dog at the helm of a tugboat
The ice on the river cracks from the strong wooden prow
As the wake parts shattered pieces
Like broken promises to a solemn vow
My frozen footsteps follow me wherever I may go
Into this night across the river to where I do not know

Old '58

I was going through the newspaper just the other day
Where I spotted an ad to sell an old Chevrolet
I made a note of the phone number as well as the price
Pictured myself behind the wheel, on the rearview mirror a pair of fuzzy dice
I called got directions from some voice that sounded old and gray
The address was out in the sticks a four-hour's drive away
I located the house someplace out east at about a quarter to nine
Strode up to the front porch, rang the doorbell, heard a chime
The door was opened slowly by a farmer I'd guess
Wore bib overalls, faded blue cap, inside looked a mess
You must be that city fella, who called about the car
Yes I replied, didn't know I'd have to drive this far
We'll she's out in the back, behind the house, stored in the barn
Haven't much time these days to drive her, it's covered up from harm
The old man tugged on a greasy and yellowed old drop
To reveal a mint four door cherry red hardtop
With white walls, thin pin stripes and chrome, bumper to bumper
My eyes opened wide, as if I awoke from a deep slumber
Don't know if she'll start up, sittin' here idle, it's been a while

Fox Tales

Here's the keys give it a run, I'll be at the wood pile
I opened the door, slid onto the rolled and pleated leather front seat
Inserted the key into the ignition and fired up the engines heat
Sensed it wanted to fly, shifted from neutral and into high gear
Eased out of the barn and stepped on the gas without any fear
I waved at the farmer as I zoomed on pass
Got a quarter of a mile down the road I was running low on gas
Made a U-turn drove back to the farm in less than a sec
Put the Chevy in park, then proceeded to write out a check
What's the price you're askin' farmer, to let her go?
Let's see he replied, she is a classic I'm sure you know
It was left here so many years before
By my dad who was in the Korean War
He came back a cripple, denied a veterans disability
The government informed him it was not their responsibility
Look I said, I'll pay you a fair buck
I'll take good care I'll call her Lady Luck
It's not the money sonny, he answered me
I sure could use the scratch you betcha certainly
It's that she's sort of sentimental you know, it has roots
Like a worn old shirt or a pair of mud caked work boots
I understand exactly where you're comin' from old man
Lost a good buddy of mine, while fighting in Vietnam
Well we sat and talked on that front porch till the sun went sour

James R. Fox

Departed shortly thereafter, I watched the farmer in the darkness of the hour
But I'll soon not forget that day till the day I die
Behind the wheel of the Old '58 man I was flyin' high
But much more than that I can honestly testify
Priceless conversation between that old farmer and I

WISHFUL THINKING

As I write upon this page with a favorite book between my knees
A cool January day outside my slightly open window allows the breeze
To chill my toes and move my thoughts along
With warmer climes to an island paradise where I belong
Fill me with rays from the sun, pleasures of endless days
Forget about the past the wherefores and who pays
Intoxicate my dreams fulfill this lonely soul
Dwell in solitude high upon a grassy knoll
Overlooking the harbor, sails billowing in the breeze
Seagulls walk the beach, old fishermen at the dock on their knees
How easy it would be to leave all behind
To escape from this city have no pretense of mind
No suitcase or carry-on for this one way trip
A few hours later, I'd be on some ship
Partaking in a happy hour, delights on the fantail
Just chillin' with the crew and passengers before we set sail
A promise, a vow I made to myself long ago
To seek comfort and joy, stow all my sorrows down below
For it matters not what course to set
But only to do it, a sure well placed winner takes all bet

Streets Filled with Broken Dreams

Candy store Mommas push their strollers filled with dreams
Drug pushin' Poppas needles inject the poison of means
Bloodstained sheets a hangin' on the clothesline roof
Cops give chase fire shots obtaining little definitive proof
From Harlem to Hollywood it doesn't matter it's all the same crap
Underwater sex, local news at six, another sleazy politician beats the rap
Greyhound bus is leavin' from Port Authority, just around noon
Heartbroken honey sits at the windowsill hopes he'll return soon
Televangelist on the screen says all of your sins will be washed away
Boom box radios blast lyrics about killin' anyone who gets in the way
Tokyo girls dressed in kimono designs of the latest Oriental fashion styles
Subway station psychos hide in the deep dark tunnels for miles
Brown corduroy jackets with torn leather elbow patches
Black and white pictures, a useless wet box of matches
Somebody's old man sittin' and sippin' alone at the bar
Who could have been a contender who might have gone far?

Fox Tales

Fire trucks, hooks and ladders, the brave in helmets and boots
Into the fire everyone died, dignitaries at their funerals in designer suits
Twenty-four hours, every day in the week, the results are often the same
The papers all lied, wasn't suicide, but justice that tarnished their great name

He & She

He was born in Manhattan, on the Upper East Side
She was born in Brooklyn separated by a subway token ride
He was the youngest child born to Pete and Ann
She was the oldest girl, born to Jack and Fran
He grew up moving to many different places
She played with dolls that had pretty faces
The first time that they met was by just a stroke of fate
He had tickets to the Rangers she went on their first date
They were happy and surprised how easy it was then
She kissed he at the subway stop, they didn't want it to end
It was shortly thereafter that he had to leave
The Navy called him, she held onto his sleeve
They dated for a while, but things started to change
Let's be friends she said, the words were cold and strange
He was stationed on a ship, at a place called Little Creek
She started to date again, week after week
He traveled to many ports, took in everything there was to see
She must have had him on her mind, she wrote to him eventually
One day while on the ship, he received her letter
She asked how he was doing she was sick but now feeling better
He went home that weekend, contemplated to give her a call

Fox Tales

She answered the phone, her voice decided it all
They got together that very night
She and he saw each other in a different light
They soon got engaged, planned their wedding day
A fight soon ensued he and she wanted their own way
He went to a bar to cool things down
She simmered at home looking at her wedding gown
The wedding took place on a warm July day
The guests tossed rice and danced the night away
They honeymooned in Montreal
Where it felt like the fall
He was still in the Navy
When came their first baby
He sailed the day before Tara was born
She kept him informed, their love still warm
By the end of the year no more Navy, he was out in the clear
With a wife and a baby girl, he was anxious with fear
They gave it a go, but at first it was slow
He drove a cab she stayed at home as the three began to grow
After a while she said to him, I feel like I'm pregnant again
Nine months later, a baby girl who they named Erin
He found himself out of work as the economy went sour
She had faith nevertheless, kept busy by the hour
He never gave up, later held two jobs and attended college at night
She tended to the girls, cooked his meals made their home just right
Then once again came a glow in her eyes, he sensed that look before

James R. Fox

He said to her no not again, we haven't room for one more
She replied guess what, it's a girl welcome Terri number three
So there they were he and she
Three daughter's one big happy family
The years went by in the blink of an eye
Their parents are gone now, missed so desperately
Visit their graves pay their respects solemnly
The girls are now grown
Pursuing dreams of their own
He and she see them every once in a while
Are proud grandparents to Benjamin, Daniel and Kyle
He and she are now older keep busy nevertheless
Watch the grandkids who tire them out they must confess
At the end of the day they kiss and say good night
He goes to bed with a prayer in his head then turns out the light
She waits just outside the bedroom door
After all this time, nothing less and nothing more
For after so many years
Filled with the laughter, filled with the tears
Once upon a time there was he and she
An attraction toward one another that was destined to be

Something Was Special That Day

Went to Strawberry Fields to see how it feels
Shortly after George had passed away
With video camera in hand, I began to scan
The oh so many faces
Songs that came so softly
Accompanied by guitars at hand
Around the mosaic titled IMAGINE
Were flowers pictures and candles
We attended in many colors
As well as attire
There were even some wearing sandals
George did that for us
And so much more
He helped turn the pages
A sage for all the ages
It was a cool crisp December day
As I moved among the crowd
I could tell that Central Park
Was filled with his love and his music
I watched the children at play
As I silently walked away
I knew that George was watching
From somewhere, so proud
My sweet Lord
You have taken George away

Fox Tales

He is finally at rest
Playing in that glorious band
With Buddy Elvis Jimi Janis and Roy
As I departed the park
Just as the sky was turning gray
I'll forever keep this day
December 1, 2001 precious
As a child with a new toy
On a new Christmas Day

Those Were the Days

Whenever I get together with the family or friend
The topic always tends to drift
To do you remember when?
So here is a list off the top of my head
In no particular order
Fay Wray, Doris Day, Johnny Ray
South of the Border
One of these days Alice
The pestle is in the chalice
Funny Loony Toons
Beatniks, pickup sticks
Saturday matinee cartoons
Leapin' lizards, we're off to see the wizard
Hey, I'm walkin' here!
Hula Hoops go go boots
Flashlight tag, Hire's root beer
The Shadow knows, Bob Hope's nose
All the Ed Sullivan shows
Bungalow Bar, the Edsel car, the Brother's 4
Watch the revolving door
The Automat, are you gonna eat that?
Well I'll eat my hat
Don't forget to vote
We're gonna need a bigger boat
Iron Curtain, the Beatles Invasion
Elvis swivels on the stage,
 Working for the minimum wage

Fox Tales

Davy Crockett's coonskin hat, Felix the Cat
See you in September, try to remember
1963 in late November
All Along the Watchtower
Defiant Black Power
The 3rd Avenue El
Call for Philip Morris
Steve Allen, Ernie Kovacs
The farmer in the dell
Palisades Park, Dick Clark
When New York lost power and was left in the dark
What me worry?
Mac & Cheese, roller skate keys
Slow down, what's the hurry?
3D glasses, attending midnight Masses
Saturday night dance
Pegged pants, teenage romance
C'mon & take a chance
Jackie Wilson, the 4 Tops
The Temps, the Miracles & the Supremes
The Platters, the Moon Glows
The gal or the guy of your dreams
Safari jackets, desert boots
James Dean's lookin' cool
Poodle skirts, egg creams, baseball cards
Everybody plays the fool
Twilight Zone, princess phone, black & white TV
Gabby Hayes, Happy Days
A slinky on the stairs
Sesame Street, Barbi dolls
Yogi & the 3 Bears

James R. Fox

So here's to you kid
I'm ready for my close up now, Mr. De Mille
Anything goes thar she blows
Some Like It Hot
House on Haunted Hill
John Wayne, Coney Island Express Train
All That Jazz, razz ma tazz
The Bronx and the Central Park Zoo
Ben Blue, a fake tattoo, nothing new
How's about you?
Does anyone but me know who said?
Wee woo I'm with you
While holding in his hand a rubber tree plant
Zacherly, Norton Nork
Name all the Monkees
Don't forget Peter Tork
Take me to your leader
Liar, liar pants on fire
I want to take you higher
The Lion Sleeps Tonight
Hop scotch, stickball, off the wall
Simon Says
Red rover, red rover
Red light green light 1 2 3
Candy Pez
Ding Dong School, the Lone Ranger
Sharing a Sky Bar
Have Gun Will Travel, the Man from UNCLE
Batman's car
Yoyos, water pistols, Bonomo's Turkish Taffy
Elmer Fudd, Bugs Bunny, Heckle & Jeckle

Fox Tales

A duck named Daffy
Schoolyard rules, Sunday best shoes
A nickel for the Mirror or the News
Musical chairs, summer camp
PF Flyers and crew cuts
The iceman, lineman
A pack of unfiltered cigarette butts
Everything is fine and dandy
Mom & Pop stores
Assorted penny candy
Captain Video, Howdy Doody
Captain Kangaroo, Andy's Gang
Amos & Andy, My Little Margie
Desi and Lucy
Cap guns, bang bang
Pogo sticks, last licks
Hide and go seek
Hello mudda, hello fadda, Sputnik
Lights Out, too scared to take a peek
Cuttin' school, shootin' pool
Kookie Kookie lend me your comb
The Battle of New Orleans
Everybody wore dungarees
Iron on patches at the knees
Poe, Frost, good thinkin' Lincoln
The Christmas tree at Rockefeller Center
Wax lips, take little sips
A hardly-ever-used fallout shelter
Moody Blues, blue suede shoes
Where the buffalo roam
Auntie M, there's no place like home

James R. Fox

Peanut butter and jelly
Mallow Mars
Chew gum, pat your head and belly
Frankenstein, I Walk the Line
Patsy Cline, the five and dime
Winky Dink, Coco the Clown
Beat the Clock
Rockaway Beach, dodge ball
Hickory, Dickory, Dock
Charlotte Ruse, Bullwinkle the Moose
Loose as a goose
Skip rope, ball and jacks, box ball
Johnny ride the pony
Fabian, Chubby Checker, Connie Francis
The sounds of Mony Mony
A little dab will do ya
Mr. Clean, Cosmo Topper
Buddy Holly, Richie Valens, the Big Bopper
Buying the latest 45's
Everybody doing the hand jive
Shindig, American Bandstand
Don't forget Hullaballoo and Hootenanny
Jed and Jethro
Season with Clampett Granny
Happy Trails, Soupy Sales
Heads or tails bang zoom
Do you have a room?
Down the drain, up the chimney
Through the looking glass
Keep off the grass
So let it be written, so let it be done

Fox Tales

Who you gonna call?
Who are those guys?
He sailed right out there
Wide gaudy ties
And the people all said sit down
I coulda been a contender
Shane, come back Shane
Top of the world ma
Hey Abbott, Oh Archie
This is a fine mess you've gotten us into
Christmas, bah humbug!
Cut a rug
Go ahead punk, make my day
Real Christmas trees
Reading tea leaves
Rock paper scissors
It was beauty that killed the beast
If I were the king of the forest
The Colonel must know
We don't need no stinkin' badges
Sgt. Bilko, Marshall Dillon
Sgt. Preston of the RCMP
I'd be remiss to omit little Rusty
All were tall big or small
Old Yeller, Lassie, Bullet and Rin Tin Tin
Well I am nearly at the end of my list
But I know there is so much more
Did I mention Davega's stores?
So here's to Willie Mickey and the Duke
Loved by all from Flatbush to Dubuque
And to all the boys of summer

James R. Fox

So I raise a glass to you
My family and old friend
To a time that shall not pass
This way ever again
For those were the days
In oh so many ways

THE INEVITABLE

Into the silent sweet night I dare to step
My passport hand delivered has long ago expired
So lovely the pipes play
An Irish reel
Mist is upon the heather, so surreal
Be kind to me stranger
For I know not
Which path to choose
For it is written, a secret soliloquy
That at the crossroads
Of death and desire
The final chapter left unread
Can never be opened
Later on the holy water
That originally cleansed our souls
Solves the question
Where we are headed
Back to where we came from
It is always a challenge
To perform a noble task
To conquer each and every fear
Accept what thou lost
The price it has a cost
So that when the last day
Finally arrives at our door
We can greet the Grim Reaper
As a Motley Fool

Grand Premiere

Places everyone, places everyone
Audience kindly locate your seats
The show will now commence
Management recommends complete and absolute silence
Throughout tonight's performance naturally
So without further ado
I give to you ladies and gentlemen
The presentation of a lifetime
The houselights dim
The maestro cues the orchestra
A spotlight brings into focus
The crimson curtain rises
The actors take their places
With panache, style and aplomb
Will the show be a smash or perhaps a bomb?
Is it a musical or a drama?
Perhaps we shall see a lighthearted comedy
The topic of conversation
During the intermission
One could not tell, for to break the spell
If it were a ballet, or an operetta
The plot would mesh so much better
Thus came part two, the actors unsure of what to do
A flourish of woodwinds and French horns
Suddenly the lights went out
Quickly followed by a loud pistol shot

Fox Tales

A gasp from the audience and the actors on the stage
The houselights promptly turned on
This is preposterous, what gall
Then came a hysterical cry
From a box seat on high just right of the stage
Oh my Lord my love, stay with me
Please don't die!
Her husband in great distress
Has blood on his chest
Slightly above his heart
How could this be?
It must be part of the play
But it was no act
But a clever ruse to distract
By an assassin after the fact
Did the show ever go on after the harm?
One can only guess
Until this very day, the play
Is in storage and locked away
As for the killer who vanished into the darkness
They say his ghost often visits this very theater
For in whispers and sighs
Cast members at times are terrified
Others scoff and belie the conclusion
A mysterious production the Grand Premiere
Which opened and closed the same night
In shock, horror and confusion

INTROSPECTION

Every day I attempt to write
Upon an empty page
My main intent
I try to invent
An expression or emotion
If I could travel as a bird
Without a word
There would be heard
No finer rhapsody
The concern of mine
Consisting of meter and rhyme
Searching ones soul and heart
Is where I shall finish
Before I begin
A spark must have a start

Half-Time

Western boots and long lasting looks captured so naturally
Grand Canyon smiles and Coney Island mermaids
Postcards sent home when left all alone
Church doors unlocked, engagement rings hocked
The butcher sharpens his knives before slaughter
The baker the banker and the guru's virgin daughter
One painted pony on the rail, nicknamed Macaroni
Fancy checkered vest, monogrammed family crest
Cashless wet bar, a chance to drive one fancy sports car
Submarine duty lookin' good
Dutch doors carved from solid wood
Newborn turnin' blue, a brand new watch for you
All the worlds a mess, nothings new why confess
That faraway look in a stranger's eyes
See what a Euro in the USA can buy
Fences being erected to quarantine the neglected
Lab rats are to blame
Billionaires lather in their self-made fame
Tinted windows of limousines expose
Nickel-plated guns, one can only suppose
Pearl divers in the South China Sea
Are paid in clam wages and dehydrated tea
Himalayan villages isolated and remote
Prayer wheels of the lamas in snow that denote
An elderly patient gasps one last dying breath
Caregivers provide one final request

Fox Tales

Age of reason and nothing more
Lessons written on a blackboard a yawn of a bore
Drain the brain one has to explore
Solve the theory and deduce the core

In the Beginning

In the beginning God created the heavens and the earth
Our Creator had an idea or a spark
God said let there be light to remove the dark
Stars were placed as constellations
A covenant of his ark
Mountains were formed in His mighty hands
Rivers and streams, oceans in place of lands
Forests of green, orchards of ripen fruits
Animals, birds and fish of the seas
Mighty redwoods and trees of deep roots
The Creator must have been lonely all by himself
So He needed another ingredient siting on the shelf
From out of clay He molded a man
Yes He said smiling I shall call you Adam
Before long God could tell Adam appeared sad
I see said the Lord you need a mate
So God created Eve from one of Adam's ribs
In Eden they dwelled until a date with fate
The serpent was shrewd knew what was in store
Take a bite of the apple Eve
Just try a little, you'll soon want more
Adam was next to the serpent's delight
The Creator had forewarned them
Exit from Eden, Adam and Eve
Be gone now, out of my sight
That was so many years ago

Fox Tales

Recorded in the Bible we all know
Chapter and verse
Could events turn worse?
Centuries flew past there was Noah in the Ark
Moses led his people through the desert
In the search of a land of milk and honey
The Holy Roman Empire ruled
Julius Caesar's image on all the money
The chosen ones the twelve tribes of Israel
Were foretold a messiah shall come
To lead them out of harm's way
It will be soon, perhaps any day
John the Baptist at the banks of the River Jordan
Was overcome with awe
As he glanced upon His face
I am not worthy to loosen your sandals lace
Jesus was sent here to take care
Of His Father's business
To raise the dead, heal the lepers
To have the blind see and to bear witness
Our Father gave His only Son
A specific amount of time
To walk on the earth, preach about love
As the Holy Spirit was present
In the form of a dove
There are forty-six books in the old
A total of twenty-seven in the new
Too numerous names to mention
A who's who of who begat who
We all come in different colors
Speak many languages as well as dialect

James R. Fox

Reside from sea to shining sea
In palaces or run down shacks
Worship in churches, temples, pagodas and mosques
Prayers unspoken in silence
Memorials to those who we have lost
Our Father who art in heaven
Thank thee for all you have given
Maker of all seen and unseen
Take us out of the shadows
Lead us through your valley
With your guiding hand
As we follow in the footsteps of Jesus
Beside the still waters
As they wash over the sand
The Holy Spirit who gives us
Guidance and inspiration
The Holy Trinity I truly believe
Is the doorway
That leads to eternal salvation

WHEN

When the last sin has been heard in confession
When life is protected at the moment of conception
When all children will be safeguarded from fear
When morals are held sacred and dear

Then tears from heaven will dry
Then angels' love will be on high
Then wars will end before being started
Then those that grieve for their dearly departed

Will join them again at the Lords request
Will be rich as a pirates treasure chest
Will experience happiness like never before
Will be safe as they enter through heaven's door

All of these things one day shall come
All of the pain and the sorrows shall be done
All of our prayers shall finally be heard
All of our thoughts are of one word

The good will know exactly where they stand
The wicked shall depart Eden and be banned
The time for the chosen to tally all of the cost
The time for non-believers to realize their loss

Heart Attack & Pain

There is a non- discreet diner on a run- down street
Directly across from Louie's pool hall where the low life all meet
I exited the number 7 on the El and walked down the stairs
The day was misty and gloomy as if nobody cares
I entered the greasy spoon found a seat at the counter table
What will you have Mac, a cup of joe freshly brewed by Mable
Coffee would be fine and a piece of lemon pie
Never saw your mug in here, are you a cop or private eye
I smiled back and replied neither I'm a reporter
Really are you here to do a story about me, you oughta
The name is Mitch I'm the owner of this here joint
Glad to meet you let me get right to the point
What do you know about the recent child murder?
It happened, just a few doors down
Yeah, that was a shame
It was her stepfather to blame
We get all types who walk through the door
If I knew what happened I'd settle that score
Do you see the two guys sitting in the booth?
There's Nicky the nose and Vince the tooth
Now nobody can say how many stiffs are floatin'
In the river who cares not boastin' just quotin'
Thanks for the heads up Mitch, oh by the way
Do you believe the papers in what they say?

Fox Tales

Nah a bunch of crap, use them to wrap the fish
Right here is where the news is don't I wish
Well I finished the coffee along with the pie
Paid the bill turned and walked out waving goodbye
I crossed to the other side of the street
Entered Saint Mary's blessed myself then took a seat
In the last pew I bowed my head
Said a silent Hail Mary for the child who is dead
Where is this world headed if we fail to protect
The little ones who take the blows out of neglect
I left the church shortly after then stopped outside her door
A shrine was erected consisting of flowers toys candles by the score
This is what occurs in the poor inner city
Everyone is to blame, isn't it a pity
Where is the justice when the accused says, it wasn't me
The child gets unruly needs to be punished don't you see
There will come a day when there will be nobody to save
We need to wake up before everyone has one foot in the grave

Requiem for Reverend Greene

I attended the requiem for the dearly departed Reverend Greene
The church was on a high hill the service was sedate and serene
The bishop was in an ornately vestment and a tall miter
The music from the organ echoed the choir voices octaves higher
The six pallbearers gathered at the foot of the altar
Relatives sat stone cold, resembled the Rock of Gibraltar
The prelate began the service with a somber sounding speech
Listing all the many attributes including the gift to teach
Describing in detail of his devout life
His loving family and his faithful wife
We shall all indeed miss him, need I say more?
Suddenly all eyes were focused on the main aisle's door
A very mysterious alluring and voluptuous woman all dressed in red
High heel stilettos on her feet matched the hat on her head
In her trembling hands she carried just a single black rose
Said the wife of all the nerve, who is she do you suppose?
How dare you, can't you see we grieve for him
You may have cared deeply but I was his whim
Whenever there was time we would secretly steal away
We made passionate love, danced laughed and hoped that someday

Fox Tales

We could leave this all behind and start fresh and anew
It is now too late for our lasting rendezvous
I had no idea, to look for telltale clues
I diligently pressed his clothes and polished his shoes
It was assumed I thought that he was busy working late
That was a ruse a perfect lie, so you were his date?
Yes it is all true no need now to be coy
He cared deeply, for you Deidra and your son Elroy
I just wanted to pay my respects then be on my way
Over my dead body I'll bet, you'll have a price to pay!
As you can plainly see there was quite a scene that day in church
Ushers intervened, fists flew the choir sang Amazing Grace,
The congregation all in a lurch
It was total chaos the funeral turned into a bloody mess
Swollen eyes, cut lips, clothes ripped, who won is anybody's guess
The last thing I remember if my memory is in place
The lasting expression on the Reverend Greene,
A smile that death could not erase

Themes of a Dream

Do not believe everything that you see and read
And less of what you hear please heed
Do not mess around where you shouldn't poke
Always act accordingly before a word is spoke
Value your friends as if treasure rooms
Keep family as rare heirlooms, Spanish doubloons
Take the time to absorb as much as you desire
Seek the truths of your mind and soul as you acquire
The proof of all the answers that we all seek
Follow in the footsteps of the prophet of the meek
Drink the nectar, a gift out of the silver cup
Allow the stranger to sit at your table and sup
Be not afraid to vanquish and to face your foes
Know that life is a path filled with highs and woes
As the last wisps of smoke ascend from the fire
May all of your secret wishes, aspire that much higher

An Air of Desperation

Is there any logic in the tonic that I take?
If I were to borrow from tomorrow a big mistake
The book is open to a page I cannot read
Where are you going, I shall not follow your lead
The local gin mill makers and the table salt shakers
The cobblers and haberdashers, errand runners the lot of them all fakers
Blackboard erasers, Lear Jet races, unwanted orphans, box loads of coffins
Epitaph of the living, alms for giving, seldom minus often
Signs in the shadows too faded to make them out
Hurricanes in the brain, where storm clouds hide any doubt
Hesitant in plaid pants, last rites removes any faint chance
Downhill climber, back door clues, we all need true romance
Ten words entered upon a line, count each one carefully
As the weather vane moves, so shall we eventually

No Destination Known

If I had the gumption I'd hop on a freight train
I'd leave a note behind as I would try to explain
The reason for leaving, maybe you know bottled up inside
So I'm taking to the rails for a little hobo ride
You see, I'm feeling kind of rusty
As if the parts are running low
I'm too tired of being dusty
A fresh start, somewhere new to go
Be it a custom made solution
Or perchance an invite to depart
That is where, my dilemma lies absolution
Where to exit once I start
Exotic islands in the Caribbean Sea
Doesn't really matter which one I'd choose
My escape plan is just for the present as I can plainly see
Soaking up the rays, enjoying a lazy midday snooze
I'd let my hair and beard grow long
Might even pick up a tattoo along the way
Watch the sunset sink below the horizon
A fitting end to a perfect Margarita day

Were You There?

Were you there at the time of Our Lord?
When Jesus wept at the Stations of the Cross
Were you there when Pilate condemned Jesus to death?
When Our Lord took His last and final breath
Did you stand in the shadows and jeer as Jesus stumbled by?
Did you mock and scorn Him when Jesus fell, where was your reply?
Did you feel for Him when Jesus fell the first time?
Did you offer your hand, wasn't His pain yours as well as mine?
Among the crowd Jesus sees Mary in tears
Amidst the sorrow the loss of a mothers fears
A Roman Centurion whips Our Lord upon His back
A stranger, Simon of Cyrene, cares where others lack
Veronica wipes the blood from the face of Our Lord
Veil of tears are gathered to be loved and adored
The Cross is weighing heavy as He falls once more
The sky is turning gray a storm is in store
Jesus speaks to the women, have compassion for one and all
Jerusalem's holy temple will be destroyed all but the Western wall
His suffering is too shocking to witness, as Jesus falls to His knees
He came to us in peace from heaven, Our Father save Him please

Stripped of His garments that now lie at His feet
Show the pain Jesus endured for souls resurrected shall meet
On the Cross that He carries Jesus is nailed to the wood
One last time Jesus cries Father I did all that I could
It took some time before Jesus finally died
In heaven and earth many eyes have cried
Eventually the body of Jesus on the Cross was taken down
Everyone walked away with blood on their hands and His thorny crown
There was a tomb set aside where Jesus was laid to rest
Three days later in heaven seated on a golden throne Jesus is the best
Fourteen Stations of the Cross, Jesus endured such a heavy load
For the salvation of our souls He walked that deadly road

Painted Ponies

Many moons ago, prior to Columbus arriving lost upon our shores
Long before the Pilgrims at Plymouth and slavery darkened our doors
On the Great Plains in the tall grass where the buffalo roam
The Indian Nations were the first to call America the beautiful their home
From the majestic Rocky Mountains to the hills of Tennessee
All along the Appalachian Trail, from sea to shining sea
The tribes followed the herds, fished and respected their Mother Earth
Survived the harsh seasons, prayed for the dead, revered every birth
Hunted the woods in search of bear, deer and moose
Pitched many teepee, where the squaw would protect their papoose
America was a vast country, once free, back in its infancy
A Garden of Eden it truly was a sight to see
The many tribes, respected each other's boundaries, seldom was there a war
The Great Father allowed for freedom, no need to settle a score
People did not own the land, it was given only temporarily

Fox Tales

Inside of all living things the spirits dwell, in peaceful harmony
On the bare backs of painted ponies, sharpened arrows in leather quiver
The braves take aim at the game, hit the targets and deliver
Provide for their family, the elderly women and men
Keep the fires burning in the wickiup's Hogan's and secluded den
It was a simple basic plan, leave every rock unturned
Now look at the world, what have we all learned?
The forests are all gone, new condos they are making
Farms are going bankrupt, easy picking for the taking
Miles and miles of concrete highways and skyscrapers by the score
The Great Father gave us everything, but we wanted much more
We erect fences keeping neighbors and outsiders off our precious property
It states so in the Bill of Rights, it grants us liberty
Promises were made that were never carried out
Signatures signed on peace treaties leave any doubt
The painted ponies at the carousel and on the merry-go-round
All the riches and wampum are worthless, only faith in God, duly bound

BLESSINGS

Count all your blessings as if they were rosary beads
List one and all as a variety of individual needs
Play close attention to each and every dream
As if a salmon swimming against the stream
Be patient if fortune does not pay a call
Far be it safe than to have lost all
Often are the days when the world appears strange
Where faces in the crowd are solemn and disarranged
So fleeting the time it seems to pass
The grains of sand inside the hourglass
Darkness creeps over my wooden floor
Evidence to cover less never more

Over the Horizon

Ahoy me hearties, get set to cast off all lines
For where we are headed we'll drink the richest wines
All the ports from here to the Seven Seas
Aye the British, the French all will clearly see
That aboard this Jolly Roger with her blackened sails
We'll bring fear in bloody boots and in dungeon jails
Any ship that tries to flee or turns to fight
A broadside of cannon power will light up the night
I was born in a raging storm off the coast of Zanzibar
Kidnapped at the age of twelve by a pirate with a scar
But I have no regrets of past evil deeds
I learned from the best, left planting my seeds
Now make haste, weigh the anchor, listen up my crew
A new moon is approaching, there is much to do
Our plundering days are ahead of us, move smartly about
Sharpen your cutlass keep the powder dry remove any doubt
If my name isn't Sea Dog, I'll hoist ye from the yardarm
Or cast ye adrift on a raft in bloody seas not calm
Destiny is ours it is there for the taking
Years from now when you are old and aching
What memories you'll conjure up and remember
A pirate's life who did not surrender
The world is ours lets sail away
Lift the gangplank without further delay
Long gone are these days of buried treasure tales

Fox Tales

Of buccaneers and mutineers who were tough as nails
If only I had the chance to set my eyes upon
Come on lets sail away you and me just over the horizon

Obituary

I heard about his passing just the other day
It made the local paper, or so they say
He was a good ole' boy that played the guitar
Fought in Nam back in '69 received the Silver Star
I met him once as I stumbled out of some hillbilly bar
In his fringed vest, cowboy hat, sitting behind the wheel of the car
He smiled and winked at me invitingly cool with the most devious grin
Need a lift, hop in take a swing of my homemade moonshine gin
It was starting to rain, so I said what the heck
Where to he asked, I don't know I forgot to check
Well we proceeded on down some lost country dirt road
Out in the sticks, where white lightning lightens the load
Shortly after that is when everything sort of turned black
Awoke the next morning with a knife blade at my back
Give me your money or I'll slit your throat
Sure no problem, I replied it's in my coat
Well no sooner than a stack of hotcakes could get cold
A crack of a bullwhip snatched the wrist so I was told
It happened so fast, it was just a blur
The thief bolted and left behind a silver spur
This happens every time I come home
The local varmints never leave me alone
I was astonished I had no words to say

Fox Tales

He picked up his guitar and started to play
A few chords or two, I remember the melody
Feed me some words kid, he called to me
Well I started humming at first, to keep time to the rhythm
Then the words seemed to flow slowly as of some spiritual hymn
That was the last time I saw him, before I settled down
When all the cobwebs, the booze, took a bus out of town
Now I sweep up the floor of this local saloon
Dreams that collect dust, all have vanished, gone too soon
Keep a quarter handy in my jeans, for help and good luck
Listen to B17 on the jukebox titled My Very Last Buck
That was the only hit that he ever made
Blew it all chasing wild women, after getting paid
I bet he's smiling somewhere, now laid to rest
He fought a good fight, I sure can attest
If it weren't for him, I'd be dead for sure
If he didn't come rushing on in, through that door
That most definitely was the highlife of my life
When a somebody, saved a nobody at the edge of a knife

IN GOD WE TRUST

I had to appear before the court just the other day
I supposedly broke the law pay the summons without further delay
How do you plead, the judge asked of me?
Guilty but I hope you will hear my plea
You see your honor I went to the local bookstore
To purchase a Bible, need I say more?
Well the manager gave me an evil look so hard
Before I knew it, I was escorted out by a burly security guard
I never felt so humiliated in my life, manhandled upon the street
I ventured to the neighborhood library surely there would be no heat
I searched high and low in locating a single Bible
We don't stock them here because we would be liable
This is what the head librarian stated, as a matter of fact
Why it's absurd no Bible to read, I was enraged to react
Then the cops arrived and I was issued a ticket
For raising a ruckus, like playing with a sticky wicket
How in the world did the minorities get their way?
As a kid in school, we were allowed to pray
Say the Pledge of Allegiance, listen to scripture and verse
Play fair, try not to lie, things could always be worse
In the assembly hall in all of the public schools
We were there to learn and abide by the rules

Fox Tales

Now it's all changed, God's name is taboo
There is no respect, burn Old Glory too
Glorify all the punks and their vile wanton ways
But they can't hoodwink me, I've seen better days
Well you've broken the law said the judge, now pay the fine
For wanting to read the good old book, hell I'll do the time
You are trying my patience, the judge sternly stated
The law is all wrong, it should be debated
After all aren't witnesses in every court sworn to testify?
Place their hand on the Bible and promise not to lie
Yes that's correct replied the judge, I have to agree
Then why is it right to deny my protected liberty?
Then the judge rapped his gavel upon the bench
You are so right this law doesn't make any sense
You are free to go said the judge case dismissed
But I wanted to add if not I'd be remiss
That one day all there shall be but rust and dust
Always count your blessings and your money, In God We Trust

The Queen Bee

I managed to latch on to a hot concert ticket for a nominal fee
From a scalper I only just met, I wish that it were for free
He is a kindly old gent
Now I'm late with the rent
The show was at the Garden, I could swear half the Village was there
Everyone had arrived in platform shoes, rawhide and with glitter in their hair
There were so many acts on the bill, it was all grand
Every seat was taken it was full, some had to stand
About halfway through the show, when the tempo went into low gear
Who should appear, that star so dear, all eyes began to tear
She was in her trademark gown
Yellow and black wearing her crown
She hadn't been seen for ages, said she just wanted to be alone
Pulled a quick getaway Greta Garbo, secluded in her Beverly Hills home
That's when she took to the booze and the pills
Needed a fix, addicted to the rush, craving the thrills
The spotlight accentuated her sexy hourglass figure
From my seat her wrinkles looked much bigger
The audience came alive, it was a beehive

Fox Tales

Once she danced to that sensual, Brazilian samba jive
It was all so cool, until that fool came onto the stage
We all forgot about him, looking so old, so thin so strange
But the Queen Bee was no fool, she really kept her cool
Started buzzing around, this was her town, it was hers to rule
All of a sudden major confusion, off in the wings
A fight broke out among the wigs, costumes and things
She's been on too long, she doesn't belong it's my turn now to appear
This didn't bode well, as you could tell, the audience now gripped in fear
The Queen Bee just smiled, that was her style
Outclassed and surpassed them all, by a country mile
This was to be her swan song, her final curtain call
Shots were fired she gasped and collapsed beneath the disco ball
The funeral was truly a day of mourning black veils hid Hollywood's face
Fifty flower cars rolled up and then entered, through the somber royal estate
The papers all said, through teary eyes I read, she really was something to see
A hive of her own, never gave up the throne, forever remains the Queen Bee

Footsteps in the Snow

The first hint of great concern
Was when he did not return
We had assumed he would come back
His regular routine that was his knack
Ever since he decided to retire
The kids all gone, a time to inspire
I guess he just had enough
Like playing cards calling ones bluff
He had few close friends, that was his choice
Expressed his love to all, in pages and voice
He always dreamed of an island hideaway
Dreaded the dark days of winter's overstay
Prayed every day for his family so dear
Wished that they could always be so near
I guess in retrospect, we missed the obvious clues
The telltale signs, the mood swings, too unfamiliar blues
We are all so preoccupied, when we were so much younger
Little time to catch your breath no need to hunger
As we age, the process allows us a chance to go slow
The door has finally opened step out, leave footsteps in the snow

Handle with Care

It must have been at the initial inspection
The artwork at the gallery raised eyebrows of deception
Of an anonymous unknown caller from afar
An accent that came from the Casbah
The one-of-a-kind items, presently in your showroom
Are cursed by the Pharaohs, stolen from the hidden tomb
This is preposterous, replied the curator, surely it's a mistake
You have been forewarned return them before it's too late
One by one the crates were carefully opened by hand
Until the final odd shaped box, it contained only sand
Suddenly the air turned stale, there was an awful smell
As if an entombed mummy had arrived straight from hell
The doors of the gallery slammed closed and were unable to unlock
Then the lights went dark, an eerily stillness hearts frozen in shock
Early next morning, just around dawn, the gallery lights dimly lit
The owner arrived, the keys to the lock unable to fit
He peered into the windows to alert the security guard
He banged on the front door, yelled and whistled hard
A uniformed officer, fresh on his rounds,
 Approached the owner with suspicion
Hands up he commanded, trying to break in he spoke with conviction

Fox Tales

Officer the owner replied, I am relieved that you are here
Something must be wrong, I cannot get in, I really fear
I am the proprietor of this famous old place
Well answered the officer, I never have seen your face
There is no time, we must get in
I feel something amiss, the time is grim
Please call for assistance I feel it would be vitally needed
Then the officer and the owner entered, they should have heeded
They were cautious of their every move, as thieves in the night
In front of the locked room, shadows cast of a flicker of light
It took the both of them to force open the door
Once inside they had no idea what was in store
Several large crates were stacked neatly in a pile
Stenciled shipping labels affixed for someplace along the Nile
What happened next is perplexing, too difficult to explain
If I revealed this to you, I'd apt to go insane
Let's leave it alone, for the curious fool
A mystery to crack, with the exact tool

Beyond the Window

Beyond the window is a world I shall never see
I can only dream and wonder what there could be
Was it something I said that caused you to leave?
Now it is too late, for you to really believe
We had everything here at our fingertips
Our hearts poetic words, upon our lips
But for one brief and fleeting moment I lost it all
You were my Cinderella who lost the glass slipper at the ball
I tried to catch up as your coach drove away
No one knew your name, there was a temporary delay
We first met in secluded shadows
Our love for one another was our secret vows
A new day was a gift for us, like something to unwrap
Those days are sadly gone, a sunrise now grips me like a trap
So many years have passed, now I am old lonely and gray
Love is for the innocent who enter and will never leave or stray

LOST

Have you ever traveled down a long and winding road?
That had no signposts, only many turns up ahead
Perhaps you were tired from carrying such a heavy load
Down an unfamiliar path all alone fearful filled with dread
For it is cavalier to presume to know it all
The pretentious trip and stumble like fools in the dark
Be on guard and take precautions to avoid a fall
As a spotted owl hunts for its prey in the deserted park
There are many chances as well as risks assumed certain
Hope is wishful thinking, keep it ever close never ignore
All the puzzle clues that we lose behind the curtain
Don the wizards hat beware the black cat at the door
Maps depict various directions north and south east and west
Use them wisely for your discretion and you'll be okay
Any great mystery should contain a red herring at best
Beware the hitchhiker who asks are you going my way?

Vespers

Out in the forest far from one's line of sight
Just as the sun sets for the night
A procession commences as every pew and seat are filled
Monks in their habits pray to have their vows fulfilled
It is a sheltered and secluded life
Free of worry and free of strife
They who have chosen a path of inner peace
Dwell in a cell the Lord within arm's reach
Some say it is a calling that comes from above
It stirs the soul it brings forth love
Hard to explain to the ordinary man
Be humble abstain from sin do the best you can
All of them come from many walks of life and careers
Thought deeply of what to cast aside a future of fears
Stow away worn excessive baggage that weighs one down
Donate all worldly possessions in exchange for a crown
With rosaries in hand they pray for one and all
In silent whispers hymns they chant to inspire the call

Profile of Persistence

I thought I had my personal house in order
Until it collapsed like a deck of cards
How naïve of me to think that I am always in command
But the face in the mirror knows only too well
Fool some of the people all of the time
Pocket the ace in a hidden place for an opportune time
Apply cologne or perfume to hide the scent of defeat
Sour notes are melodious to the deaf ear
One in need of a coat on a homeless night
Doesn't pay too much attention to labels
Closing time is right after happy hour
The undertaker accepts Visa, Master Card and American Express
You can even pay off the bill by direct deposit
Street corner hustlers vie for your attention
Pass the hat and leave their guitar case open for donations
Somewhere out there far on that highway road
In the darkest of night with nothing in sight
A soul searches for a token friend
The scarecrow reaches out in a field of silence
Where rainbows collect tears of rain

Paying Respects

Sometimes when you visit us, we are covered
With a fresh blanket of new fallen snow
Other times birds stop by to build a nest and grow
We were there when you took that very first step
You were so confident full of energy and so much pep
Now we are gone just memories and dust
Faded photographs relics now covered with rust
One wonders, where all the years have gone, seemed to fly
   by
The births, christenings, graduations, weddings, sky high
Through laughter and tears of joy and fear
As you whisper their name they stop to hear
Now you are on your own, master of your fate
We are so proud of you, life is good and great
Just a reminder, as you turn off the light
Even though now we are gone and out of sight
One day perhaps tomorrow we shall meet again
To have for all eternity to reminiscence,
Do you remember when?

For Another Time

I place things on the back burner, where I know that they can sit
It may take some time, but I'll eventually get to it
Usually, I'm just too darn busy to do it right now
Feel like an old farmer, hitching a stubborn mule to a plow
Chores get in the way, when it could be great to just chill
Take the phone off the hook, and do what you will
Sure you say, but what about demands and responsibility?
Hey, don't look for me for any answers I'm the last you'd want to see
I can't decide what to wear, if my socks are an even match
Did I do that, gray in my hair, comes with the territory patch
So here's a tip, when things get a little crazy
Imagine yourself relaxing, in a hammock so free so lazy
Forget your cares and woes, bills to be paid and such
They'll always be there, some less, others much
It's been this way ever since Adam and Eve
When they went window shopping, inside of Eden and wouldn't leave
Invest your time with the talents you possess
Sip it slowly like a cup of tea, I guarantee it will alleviate all of your stress

Closing Time

It was raining I was cold and wet on an unfamiliar street
I heard footsteps behind, ducked into the nearest bar to avoid the heat
It was closing time about a quarter to three
The bartender was all alone it was just him and me
I shook off the water from my raincoat and hat
Cased the room just in case found a stool and sat
We made eye contact then came the usual, what will you have Mack?
I needed a smoke more than a drink I just emptied my last pack
Name your poison he suggested, where do I begin?
We got ryes, whiskeys, vodka, rum and gin
A glass of Chablis, sangria, a Rhine wine
That sounds good anyone of those would be fine
There are also ales and beers on tap
A few of them and you'll be taking a nap
Have you been tending bar a long time?
You could say it's been a while, what you see is all mine
I bet you see all types of people that are in need of a drink
For the most part they're all just passing through I think
So if someone had no place to go, would they wind up here?
Would you listen to their tales of woe, as they nursed their beer?
A bartender's occupation is kind of like a shrink and a priest

Fox Tales

Everyone's got a line of bull to say the least
I noticed the time on the clock it was shortly after four
Guess I better be going what's the hurry, stay for just one more
I have to confess, the bartender needed the company more or less
Don't remember leaving the bar, how I got home is anybody's guess
Early in the morning as I awoke in a haze
Fire engines with sirens tore past my house heading for a blaze
Later that evening I watched the local news
It reported the incident a bar torched no survivors just a pair of old shoes
Was I the last to have seen the bartender alive?
We never told our name, just shared small talk inside that dive
Guess what I'm saying is whose footsteps did I hear?
Who was following me, what was there to fear?
I've been sober now, going on a few months
I still get the fever sure, the itch and the grunts
But my last sip I took at the bar with that unknown fella
Now my choice of drink is nothing stronger than sarsaparilla

Searching for You

Through the passageways and tunnels of my mind
Past the locks and bolts and heartaches that bind
In reflections of a glass that mirrors the past
On a ship without a crew or a sturdy mast
I have researched all the libraries and museums
Investigated for minutest clues, retraced all of my dreams
Hiked in the park, just before sunrise
Sat on the beach trying to recapture the moonlight in your
    eyes
If there could be a semblance of a chance
To pay the piper once again then to dance
It would take a wheelbarrow filled of yesterdays
Thespians performing comedies, tragedies upon endless
    ways
In a studio of an artist where the light enters ever so slight
A colorful palette of pastels, applied to a canvas of white
The notes to a composer's trained and talented ear
That completes the movements to his sonata ever so clear
All of these things and so much more
Could never contain what is placed in a bottle to reach a
    distant shore
Simple words of love that arrives on a beach
Searching for you, I pray one day, I shall again reach

It's About Time

Semaphores of metaphors sent by Little Orphan Annie
Saturday matinee cartoons, faces consumed with cotton candy
Calypso rhythms being heard on the back porch swing
Teenagers madly in love, a future diamond engagement ring
Assorted kites flying hiding behind low lying clouds
Wet clothes drying on the line portraying weeping shrouds
Buds are sprouting in the garden, a sign of things to come
Robins build a nest for their young in the new morning sun
Bacon frying in the pan, two eggs over easy
Coffee perking, bread is toasting, love my omelets cheesy
Buffing up my blue suede shoes, pressing off an old silk tie
Carnival tents at the county fair, blueberry and pumpkin pie
Pickup trucks with bales of hay, kids playing hide and seek
Skinny-dipping in the pond, curious eyes spy a quick peek
Once upon a time we weren't concerned about the news
Who was doing what to whom or the latest views?
All that mattered was in our own backyard
Everything in our hands sometimes easy sometimes hard
We knew about the weather by the shift in the wind
Accepted the consequences, paid the fine, all accounted for who have sinned
So I'll keep my opinions to myself as I rock in this old chair

Fox Tales

Let the chips fall where they may, as if I really could or should care
All that matters is to treat each and every one as vintage wine
Family and friends grow together as fruits on the vine, until it's about time

His Voice

Is that your voice I hear oh Lord, calling out my name?
Is it time to leave, or do you want me to remain?
Have you set a place for me, in your mansion on the hill?
Do you have plans for me, perhaps a task to fulfill?
You do not know the hour or the day when the Lord will appear
It states so in the Bible, get your house in order do not fear
Lord I am not worthy, I am afraid I let you down
I am but a sinner not a saint, who wants to wear a heavenly gown
At times I feel that you are present in my thoughts and in my deeds
There are moments when it is hard to comprehend, providing basic needs
Why the poor are still unfed, why the homeless have no beds
Why is it that children and the elderly suffer for the lack of meds?
A voice is heard in the wilderness of a newborn baby's cry
Who is there to help is there no one who will even try?
I can only hope and pray that those that suffer will be heard
Please Lord hear your people, they trust and believe your every word
And so I wait for the calling of the day when it shall come
To walk into the light and see familiar faces in heaven each and every one

The Celtic Fair

Is it the essence of your warm inner glow that forever haunts me?
Or is it the mist upon the lake that I wish to forever see
The many shades of green from field to meadow bloom
No other place is it like it surely beneath a harvest moon
Oh the pipers and the fancy dancers, ribbons and bows of such
The pretty poses, eyes a twinkling, enough to make one blush
Come now, don't be shy, I see you want to join in
Our voices may be a wee bit off key we aim to please not win
All the clans are assembled here, each and every year
Telling all the folklore tales, sharing secrets, drinking beer
Aye the Irish they are scattered like seeds upon the wind
But their roots are on the Emerald Isle, calling them back home again
So no matter where ye may roam, at sea or ashore
One day you will find wonderful things there and oh so much more
For it is a magical place, filled with lies as well as truths
You'd be surprised therein that dwells a family with Irish roots

Ghosts of Power

A soldier fights in the desert against an enemy he never knew
Senators on Capitol Hill pass new laws only to hurt me and you
Messages fly along unseen wires far and wide
Clandestine events, spy to spy try to, run and hide
The sun shines on only one half of the globe
While the moon beams for the rest a nighttime bulb
Basic beliefs, common sense, knowing what to do
Number one best sellers are soon found out to be untrue
Authors caught with their hands covered in plagiarist ink
Claim for an alibi, it's not what you think
Everyone fabricates, every now and then
No need to be inventive contract clauses constantly changing again and again
When did everything start to go sour?
Was it shortly after the witching hour?
Now it seems we all possess shadows of doubt
Of those who lead, have not a clue what it's all about
The wealthy among us are groomed as rare pedigree
Attend the finest schools ignore all the rules, gratis and for free
Wake up each morning in satin and silken sheets
Their days are consumed with lies, deceits and cheats
An observer spoke some time ago, if I can recall what he said

Fox Tales

Don't believe everything you hear, and half of what is read
How many times can a bear circle a tree?
Before it realizes it is chasing its tail stung by a bee
We all share this place on a tiny blue marble traveling through space
When we get our ticket punched all depends, on the outcome of the race

Half Past Desire

Darkness looms beneath the ruins of the tombs
Shortly before the birth of a new day
Torn tapestries hide the misery displayed in empty rooms
An albatross finds shelter on a peaceful bay
Documents verify proof of where events have taken place
Flowers held in wrinkled hands of romantic days so long ago
Snow angels in winter now nothing more than a trace
Bountiful fields that used to yield never again to sow
Workers hands producing and creating, wonderful new things
Rivers ever flowing, mountains so mighty, psalms forever in awe
Children playing, laughing, singing, what great joy it brings
There lies the truth, where once were only moments, never more

IF

If I knew my days were numbered and I was running out of time
I would want to tell everyone I knew that everything is fine
Might drop in on an old friend who is on the mend
Make that last important call or drive around that last bend
Give my love a hug and thanks for all you've done
The good and bad times sometimes lost many times won
Dreams I know that will never be achieved
What could have been for me shall never be grieved
If my last tomorrow would turn out to be today
I would want you to know before I went away
That all the gladness in my life the drops of morning dew
Fill me up knowing all the love I never knew
A life grows with roots planted deep below
The sun provides warmth gives the soil a glow
You have always been my champion all I could ever hope to be
No finer gift the Lord could ever have given me

The Mask

There is a clown who hides behind a mask
Who performs so well is up to the task
There is a writer who is in need of a plot
Piles of manuscript ideas he once so long ago forgot
There is a sculptor who creates in stone
On a scaffold high above and on his own
There is a painter who dabs in only shades of blue
A canvas sits on an easel torn not new
There are those among us who never take the time
To take a closer look to listen to the rhyme
Who only pay the price then politely turn away
Fail to investigate what others have to say
Are always conscious of the dance
But too timid to ever take a chance
Hide their eyes from strangers in the street
Afraid what may be construed if they should meet
So they hurry in the dark to their safe and secure room
With key in hand they open then lock their tomb
There they take off the mask that sets them free
Where they can be who they wish to be

NUMBERS

Upon investigating the clues in the wee small hours before dawn
The detective deduced that the remains were that of a fawn
As if not perplexing enough were no motives or signs
Sheer imagination transfixed behind hidden blinds
The foxhounds follow the scent of their prey
As horsemen take up the chase without delay
Tally ho they cry over meadow and lane
Shadows appear the hunt was all in vain
On the day before tomorrow
Will it be necessary to beg, steal or borrow?
Shall the church steeple's bell be rung?
Will the executioner's song be sung?
It would be easier if put first to a test
What the outcome would decide what was best
But who would rule true between just me and you
Simply turn the hourglass over and start anew
It may seem so sincere to cherish loved ones so dear
For whom would you choose knowing you may lose one so near
Now you may wonder if this makes any sense
Like walking barefoot on a splintered old fence
Good tidings I say as I walk away I bid you a final adieu
Who am I you may wonder, why I haven't the faintest clue

A Toast to You

There shall never be a more auspicious time
To raise my glass to toast family and friends of mine
To be like King Arthur with his knights at the Round Table
More nobler a feast could ever exist or enable
For this is our finest dazzling perpetual hour
We are so alive as if a budding exotic flower
I shall never want to take you for granted
It would be foolish and underhanded
There are days so busy lest we forget
Where royalty remains words are silent and yet
Perhaps by force of habit or mere curiosity
We close our hearts with animosity
The ones closest to us never feel the love they need
So gallant is the white knight upon the steed
Who shall slay the dragon and save the damsel in distress
They shall always remember the day but never confess
So before another day disappears to be never more
Our time together is worth more than a vault could ever store
Indeed all of this shall one day pass away
Words upon this page can never contain all I want to say
Just this but a single moment in space
Out of all you are the one there can be no better place

Chic to Chic

When it all began is difficult to tell
Like throwing coins down a wishing well
It is easier to see through springtime leaves
Than to make up excuses for do over peeves
A parallel view for uptown news
The snobs in their open toed shoes
Observe the masses behind fancy shaded glasses
Spend a fortune tattooing permanent eyelashes
These are the times that seem to flutter on by
Stories are everywhere use your net to capture the butterfly
Another suggestion if you care to hear
Are pictures snapped that never disappear
Collect all precious memories in your mind
Be able to recollect reminisce and rewind
In a dark hazy bistro where jazz once was played
Couples sip their drinks and romance is heard
Double breasted suits and polka dotted ties
Ladies in elegant dresses and ruby red lipstick sighs
Eyes all dotted and tees all crossed
Glances all around lost but never tossed
Neat as a stickpin in a dapper lapel
Sporting a fedora, made the gent look real swell
A shave and a five and dime shoe shine
Rouge on the cheeks and nails polished oh so fine
Fox stoles trailing behind stacked high heels

Fox Tales

Chauffeurs at the curb biding time for the big wheels
Everything so exciting being in black and white
A night on the town years ago a film noir delight

Now Is the Hour

Now is the time for it shall never pass
The words from the Bible recited at Mass
When we are called to stand and deliver
Tend to your neighbor as a caregiver
Jesus has carried our cross for way too long
We are the ones who now need to be strong
For the swift never tarry or show any fear
Keep their emotions in check ever so near
Strangers may come into our lives for many reasons
Tell tall tales that accumulate as the four seasons
But every once in a while chance may give you a wink
Stop you dead in your tracks to ponder and blink
We need each other in this travel along the road so long
Before we can eternally rest and hear the heavenly angel's song
I thank you for being there to listen to my every word
Prayers ascend like ashes seen as well heard

Eyes of Wonder

Raise me up to the mountaintop
Let me gaze in wonder never to stop
Shower the world in your radiant glow
Everything you have given us in love to grow
Cast upon the waters a net to calm the tide
A sea of tranquility our arms open wide
May the drums of war forever never again to be heard to kill
But instead a future testament as a beacon on the hill
Hammer all the swords into plowshares let enemies there be no more
For the Lord is soon expected tidy up and open the door
We have fought among ourselves for so many years
Split hairs of indifference a Tower of Babel built with picayune fears
Follow the children as they play with each other
Listen to their laughter as it touches father and mother
We are all but a seed that has been planted by the Creator's hand
It is up to us to either blossom and grow or wither in the sand

SIDE BY SIDE

Before it gets way too late
Beyond words or serious debate
Let's just put our differences aside
Saddle up our horses set out for the Great Divide
We have come way too far
To let it all go stale like cheap whiskey at the bar
So why don't we just shake, one another's hand
Get rid of the dust from this road of sand
I'll borrow a chapter from Lash LaRue
Crack my whip slice the jack of spades in two
Our pearl handle pistols gleaming in the sun
Every hombre that sees us will know their days are done
As we ride out just before sundown
Silhouettes shall follow us a legend renowned
They will sing songs and tell tales as well
Of the outlaws who fought the devil and lived to tell
Heroes are just memories now witnessed by only a scarce few
Their ghosts still haunt old Boot Hill they're waiting just for you

Ominous Skies

Heavy clouds are assemblin' like troops ready for a fight
It is time to get a movin' while there is still light
Oh the winds will soon be a churnin' fussin' and such
Just as soon as the screen door a closes, it doesn't matter that much
Be quick now, tend to the animals lead them straight into the barn
Hush up I say, quell their fears of any harm
We've been tendin' to this God forsaken land
Handed down from grandpa and his forefather's hand
We've tended to a few births and deaths now and then
Fought a few battles, got bruises and scars way back when
Sure as the oldest oak tree bends from the fury of the wind
Lightning bolts will strike this land time and again
For it will come to pass as sure as I'm standing here
There will be droughts and good harvests year after year
Be foolish to listen to a forecast when my eyes can still clearly see
I'll sit by the potbelly stove until the storm passes by me
It's a circle I'll tell you, in all shapes and things
Like snakes that slithers and other God's creatures who have wings
But I haven't got time to sit and chew the fat
I've got a hundred or so chores that need attention at the drop of a hat
There's a ton of tasks to do before I'm all a through

Fox Tales

So take care now you hear, stay well, here's thinkin' much
　　about you

In Heaven

In heaven there are no tears
All the angels defend against fears
The children in God's kingdom are safe
To play freely in a wonderful place
No more harm or hurt shall ever befall upon them
For there will be an eternity of joy without amen
We will never comprehend or ever know why
There are sorrows for many who obey and try
While others have it easy and live wanton ways
Their desires are foolish that lead to a path of dreadful days
But blessed are they who do care
For they shall be rewarded God's presence is everywhere
We are all just passing through on our journey home
Do not fear you are never alone
Thoughts words and deeds are duly noted
Just as surely as all the saints in heaven have voted
We are all God's children of color and race
It is up to all to make our world a better place

I'm Full of Poison Because of You

I'm sharpening all the knives in the kitchen drawer
Loadin' all the bullets into daddy's big old .44
There's not a drop of blood runnin' through these veins
Should have left ya sooner if I had any brains

It's way too late to cut the cards or spin the wheel
These scars that you made will take years and years to heal
I've done everything I could what more can I do?
I'm full of poison because of you

I'm too tired and fed up from bein' called trailer trash
Now I'm flat broke from payin' your bail of your latest pickup crash
You've been out every night lately with a new alley cat
Come home smellin' of booze and wearin' that raggedy baseball hat

It's way too late to cut the cards or spin the wheel
These scars that you made will take years and years to heal
I've done everything I could what more can I do?
I'm full of poison because of you

I'm tired and tuckered out most of these days
Oh Lord can't you see there has to be better ways
To get over you but before I'm all through

Fox Tales

I'll never stop hidin' all these black and blues

It's way too late to cut the cards or spin the wheel
These scars that you made will take years and years to heal
I've done everything I could what more can I do?
I'm full of poison because of you

9-30-55

I remember the day so vividly yet so far away
Heck, as if it were just yesterday
It was awful hot, in the middle of the afternoon
Tires squealin' kickin' up gravel like bein' tossed from a spoon
I never in my life have ever seen such a sight
A two-seat racing car, not much taller than my height
The driver pulled on in to my daddy's filling station
Fill it up kid, where the hell are we, can you tell us the location?
You're not far from Cholame on the way to Bakersfield
As I proceeded to wipe the road from the dirty windshield
The driver was brown and tan from the sun
His passenger appeared strange was quiet as a nun
Gee mister, I never seen a car such as this
Someday I'll have a fast car, boy do I wish
Well kid, maybe if you're lucky, just like me one fine day
A shiny silver Porsche 550 Spyder will come your way
The driver cleaned his sunglasses with his sleeve
If I only knew what would happen next, I would have never let him leave
But there are reasons why events happen the way they unfold
Last thing I recall was seein' number 130 tear down old highway road
Later that evening as I was kickin' stones in my worn and

Fox Tales

    torn shoes
The radio was playing Buddy Holly's Peggy Sue when we heard the news
There was a fatal auto crash at the intersection of routes 466 and 41
The deceased name was James Dean
 The cause of death was speed, often takes the young
Just twenty-four years of age who had everything right in front of him
Maybe it was the suns glare or being on an unfamiliar road
That distracted Jim
One will never know the answer we can only surmise, I guess to say
Now that I am older than the boy I was that day
I will never forget that smile, that cool blink of his wink so real
All the great roles he played, James Dean never died
He'll always be the real deal

HANDS

There are working hands that built our ancestors home
They nailed the rails sea to sea beside where the buffalo roam
There were the hands that sewed our first ragged flags
There are the hands that heal our pets a thankful tail that wags
There are hands that deliver life and others that console
Little hands that create with Mom a tasty casserole
When man walked on the moon hands planted Old Glory in place
By the grace of God His hands hold all of us a universe of space
There are the farmers who work with hands that toil
From sunup to sundown they cultivate the soil
The poets and the writers who place words to inspire
The hardhat construction workers building skyscrapers to go higher
The clowns and tightrope walkers who always rate a hand
The magicians who amaze us a precision marching band
The doctors who relieve our stress and our aching pain
The firefighters and the police who face danger but yet remain
The parents who rock the cradle to soothe the newborns fears
The newlyweds holding hands wiping away their joyous tears

Fox Tales

The hands that held our first bike and taught us how to ride
When we took our first tiny steps to waiting hands so filled with pride
As youngsters we captured lightning bugs placed them inside a Mason jar
You see our hands really do indeed tell the world exactly who we are

Cast Ye Stones Along Desolation Road

Oh ye cast stones along desolation road
Fire at Will and Suzy Phil and Jane
Let the slingshots fly then reload
Do your friends and enemies feel the pain?
After all our words are just that, they are not a big deal
Everyone is so uptight filled with stress
When they are saddened how does it feel?
But the pompous, the egoists never could guess
That the basic ideals to care for one another and console
These emotions were created and formed within the womb
Thus we must end hatred let peace be our goal
Have we not heard that Jesus has left the tomb?
Yet today we still do not heed the words
Does anyone care has it all been in vain?
All that shall be one day a migrating flock of birds
Dreams scattered upon desolation road never to be attained

Ribbons of Respect

Amid a sea of humanity
All colors of skin I see
Rows and rows fill the street
Strangers all arrive to meet
A funeral procession of plain wooden coffins
Sounds of sobbing a city lost as orphans
We come together to console and to pray
Perhaps our enemies will take notice and say
So this is the reason America is truly great
For all religions are respected no need for debate
While our children are fighting in the Middle East
It is all so pointless what matters the least
A moment in time that took so many lives away
Now a burnt out home is all that remains today
I wonder why this particular tragedy has affected us so deep
We are all connected our emotions should never be asleep
There can never be anything more precious on Earth
Than children who fill our lives from the moment of birth
So when they are taken through no fault of their own
Our faith is tested for we know not the unknown
We must show each other compassion a time to heal
Support one another honor how they feel
Every act of kindness is an example of love
This is what defines us a gift from above

Just Asking Kindly Ponder This

Have you ever seen a politician walk a union picket line?
Have the hungry ever been invited to their home to wine and to dine?
Either party the elephants and donkeys both are exactly the same
They point fingers and accuse but never accept the blame
New laws are enacted to protect them and for us to enrage
They give themselves inflated raises but won't increase the minimum wage
Americans need health insurance and a secure pension plan
While Congress twiddle's their thumbs and say we'll get to it when we can
Billions are being spent borrowed to fight the current war
Our family friends and neighbors are dying today tomorrow many more
The fat cats belly up to the bar as swine in a pen
While factories mills farms and companies close never to open again
The government is a millionaires club where the dues are a tax write off claim
The past and present presidents are masters
 Who know precisely how to play the game
How many skeletons must be in their family closets I can only guess?

Fox Tales

You see they are the masters we are the pawns
 In their never-ending game of chess
We arrived here in many different ships but now we are all in the same boat
The choice is yours or so they say trust me please I need each and every vote
Our liberty and our freedom are being chipped away a little bit each day
In the definition of eminent domain you could lose your home
 Get out of the way
I care for America of the red white and blue a mosaic of grand design
If we are not all vigilant our flag will be replaced
 With a corporate logo dollar sign

Play the Pipes and Beat the Drum

Play the pipes and beat the drum
Oh sons and daughters from Ireland ye have come
To march, down the green line with faces of pride
As generations afore have sacrificed and died
A sea of banners and colors so true
The cool crisp air the sky azure blue
From Kerry to Cork they strut all along
On the streets of New York tis where they belong
These families of the famine who dared to dream
Arrived on our shores the land of riches and cream
Churches school hospitals they built in record time
Contributed so much, a heritage of music artists poets of rhyme
We of Irish roots a mystical isle that beckons from afar
So here's to you I raise me glass a toast of who ye are

The Eve of Christmas

Twas the eve before Christmas as I fell off to sleep
Soon I was in Dreamland but I wasn't counting sheep
I found myself waking in an unfamiliar bed
Outside in the street I could hear the sound of a sled
Today it is Christmas ah yes the twenty fifth of December
The best day of the year I still do remember
But where exactly am I how
At this hour right now
It is, so bitterly cold as I throw off the covers
My bare feet touch the floor numb as forlorn lovers
Into the hall I grope the walls as I make my way
As my sore aching bones adjust for the day
In the main room I see a high back chair a pair of slippers but for whose feet
Beside is a fireplace the remains of ashes with only a trace of heat
I pass by a mirror but I do not recognize the face
Why that couldn't be it is not me my hands slowly begin to trace
I have been transformed back into another place another time
Christmas, bah humbug fit for a fool just another nursery rhyme
Who needs stockings stuffed with toys?
Gifts beneath a tree for little girls and boys
I'd rather have coins in my pockets that jingle
Than believe in a fat man in a red suit named Kris Kringle
Ah yes all that much better less cards to send

Fox Tales

Paying for stamps and postage all for a family member
 Or an ungrateful friend
Good will to men throughout the year
Just leave me alone I say let me enjoy my solitude you hear
Just then I was startled from my dream I suddenly awoke
My eyes hardly open beside me in bed I felt a tiny poke
Daddy wake up Santa was here
Tiny hands pulled at me on tiptoes I followed my eyes still unclear
A Christmas tree of blinking lights candy canes rows upon rows
Gifts of assorted boxes wrapped in pretty paper and bows
Stockings hang on the mantle filled with candy and toys
Music fills the air with Yule time joys
I am so blessed by the spirit of giving
Only miserly old men who thought their way of living
Was to turn a cold shoulder and to shun one and all
As they count their money but who shall they call
So now I raise a glass with these words for a toast
What would Scrooge do now brooding all alone?
 Sipping tepid tea with morsels of a cold mutton roast
So now on this eve before a new Christmas day
When the children are snuggled in bed listen for the bells on Santa's sleigh
We celebrate the birth of the baby Jesus a gift for me and you
Believe in Christmas, Saint Nick and most of all
 May all of your wishes come true

END TO END

Listen to this all who prophesy with your pen
Who think their world will never come to an end
You think that we will never find out
For you are mistaken fancy words filled with doubt
So type with your fingers until they bleed
For better to have than never to need
As you awake to a sunrise in your mansion on a hill
Far from the despair where one must decide food or a pill
As you constantly appear, an image all a glow
An orator of lies who presumes no one will ever know
This world of our that continues to spin
Do you have to ask what time zone you are in?
So as you pass among the lepers in the street
Rush now hide your face in case you should meet
The hour is late no time for a last kiss or fond adieu
The poet shall always tango in the moonlight with dejavu

I'll Take You In

Give me your poor, who have no home
Give me those lost, who constantly roam
Give me your sick, the abandoned in masses
Give me those blind that have lost their eyeglasses

Allow me to feed, the hungry and such
Allow me to set a table, though I haven't too much
Allow me to clothe, with a warm coat or sweater
Allow me to do this, until they feel better

Our families are hurting, day after day
Our voices cry out, there must be a better way
Our leaders all promise, they can fix this recession
Our world is in the dark, as we await the funeral procession

We are all in this together, as a matter of fact
We need to mend fences, unite as a pact
We all must weather, this economic hurricane
We will need each other, to endure the pain

So before the final, last hell's bell tolls
So before we are shipwrecked, upon perilous shoals
So before we become orphans, with no horizon known
So before all of this, love one another from soul to the bone

Thirty Pieces of Silver

Under a full moon, in the garden, Jesus began to pray
Father in heaven, give me the strength show me the way
Out from the shadows, Judas suddenly appeared, like a snake coiled to hiss
Jesus my brother, it is I Judas, as he gave Him a kiss

For thirty pieces of silver, Judas traded his soul
He gave up Jesus for a few coins, Judas dug his own hole
How could someone so close, commit such a sin?
Ask and it will be answered, knock and I'll let you in

Jesus was arrested for a trumped up charge of blasphemy
Pilate wanted none of this I wash my hands so all can see
They gambled for His garments, His only possessions, nothing more
Placed a crown of thorns upon His head, they whipped His back raw

For thirty pieces of silver, Judas traded his soul
He gave up Jesus for a few coins, Judas dug his own hole
How could someone so close, commit such a sin?
Ask and it will be answered, knock and I'll let you in

Who would betray their best friend or true love?
For some earthly rewards, tempted from below not from above

Fox Tales

Our sins and transgressions hurt Jesus just the same
We as well as Judas, must all share the blame

For thirty pieces of silver, Judas traded in his soul
He gave up Jesus for a few coins, Judas dug his own hole
How could someone so close, commit such a sin?
Ask and it will be answered, knock and I'll let you in

All Hallows Eve

Oh I have a yarn to spin, so pull up a chair
It happened a long time ago, when I had more hair
I remember a short cut home, as it was getting late
Soon I was in the cemetery, when I heard a creaky gate
I was frozen where I stood my heart was beating so fast
This can't be happening it's only a dream surely it won't last
The wind began to howl through the many spooky trees
A chill crept up my back, something grabbed at my elbows and knees
The moon was full, as shadows began to appear
I had no voice to call for help I was in a state of fear
Suddenly I was surrounded by a group of hideous ghouls
All shapes and all sizes, gargoyles, jesters and fools
Although I could see them, they were oblivious to me
How did they materialize from the graves, who dared to set them free?
My question was shortly answered, as a cold mist soon covered the land
A witch dressed all in black, began tossing colored sand
This is the hour for the dead to play
Hurry now we haven't much time for any delay
All Hallows Eve is a celebration of joy
When goblins go trick or treating as a girl or a boy
Now take to the highways, the paths and the streets
Speak not a word especially to strangers in sheets

Fox Tales

Be back before sunup or when you hear the rooster crow
Scatter like dust in the wind, now off you go
Next thing I knew I was outside my home
Would soon be visited by those who forever roam
So this is my story I relate it at this time every year
Keep a jack o' lantern in your window and you'll have
    nothing to fear

Through a Grandfather's Eyes

God must have been thinking whom shall I send
To be a grandson who I could befriend
Someone who will look different in shade of color
Who will be handsome and love his mother
Kyle is his name and teaches me something every day
He wrote of the Irish arriving at Ellis Island as an essay
I often wonder how Kyle feels deep inside
He will go far I'm filled with intense pride
Then years flew by when Kyle became a big brother
To a new baby boy named Daniel so fair
He has big blue eyes a bunch of teeth and blonde hair
Daniel has special needs can be a handful at times
Enjoys certain things that don't flow or rhyme
Kyle and Daniel are separate in many ways
Age and looks are obvious but are on the same page
They are so closely connected like left and right
So when I stop to wonder and think
What was God thinking as He gave me a wink
And just like I was gifted with three girls
All dressed in frilly dresses and curls
Along came another bundle of a surprise
Baby Benjamin grandson number three hi guys
He knows how to communicate by sign
A full house of Gods grand design
For God gave me three special gifts worth more than gold

Fox Tales

He keeps me busy with Kyle Daniel and Ben so I don't grow old
So many wonders if only I stop look and listen
We are created in many colors all included no one missin'
There will come a day when these hands will no longer be busy
I'll miss the days when the three of them drove me dizzy
I never had the chance to hold either of my grandfather's hand
To climb into their lap and try to understand
What made them happy and what made them sad
Now I am a grandfather, I can thank God for being so glad

Alter-Ego

Once again I am venturing out to sea
No more will you see my shadow any more
Far from the highways or the crooked byways
The GOING OUT OF BUSINESS sign store
I shall set my direction for the far horizon
Where the rainbow never sets
To pass the time I'll master chess
I'll even place and cover all bets
Wherever the endless waves, the cool breeze in the sails
The colorless moon of day, the ancient mariner tales
Tacking around the Tropic of Capricorn
Bow to stern my vessel adrift at the Equator
Far better to have been a sailor than never to be worn

Has Been
Could Have Been

Who was it that placed the Hollywood sign?
That attracted the starlets, the debutantes
Away from the five and dime
The allure the seduction for the busboys
The split-shift assembly line

Who was it that promised?
The keys to open the doors
But left you alone and for dead
Who carried your corpse?
From the abused empty bottles
Of the pills and the booze
That lie scattered in the heart shaped bed

Who was it that made it so clear?
Just sign on the bottom line
Then relax we'll be in touch
As you waited by the phone
For the call that never came
So attracted as a moth to the flame

Who was it that laid the roses?
On the cold unmarked grave
Who knew only to take?
But never, ever gave

Fox Tales

Who was it that stayed too long?
That lost the chance upon the hill
Who followed a dream?
That turned out to be only
A memory long last of a cheap thrill

Who was it that picked up the trash?
From Times Square after the New Year's Eve bash
Every eye from here to there
Watched as the ball came down
Out with the old and in with the new

Who was it that said?
I can't wait any longer
Time is not waiting on me
So I'll search out my fate
Before it's too late

Who was it that fell?
Way too soon
Their star shone so bright
Now only faint reminders
Of faded photographs
 Shot in black and white

Soles of the Souls in Heaven

When you see the soles of the souls in Heaven
Then you will know that the end is near
For they will all be watching from above
As they wipe away rivers of tears

When the light of day turns into night
And we can no longer see
Who will we turn to?
Who will we run to?

There have been so many prophets
Who, have warned us
Of the impending doom
But we turned away from God

It is impossible to rub away
Our sins with sandpaper
There are no antidotes to take
The poison out of our veins

So when Gabriel blows the trumpet
On the last and fateful day
The faithful and the grateful
Shall bow down and pray

Fox Tales

As the winds turn cold in winter
And the moon casts a glow
Take heed of such signs
From above as well as below

When we have read all the papers and the books
When we have witnessed all to be seen
Then all are winners regardless of their looks
Then the last, will finally be first and the first shall be last

Au Revoir

All the haunts are gone now
So where is a ghost to go?
There once was a coffeehouse
Where the poets would play chess
The floor was swept daily
Sawdust covered the stains
Magazine racks stood as sentries
Beside the barrels of pickles and peanuts
The room was filled with tobacco smoke
And the air was filled with debate
A clock on the wall chimed on the half-hour
And none were in a hurry to leave
Behind the counter were apothecary glass jars
That held peppermint and assorted chocolates
The clerks wore aprons and pencils behind their ears
For warmth in the corner was a potbelly stove

But those days have moved on
And all those that once lived are now deceased
The poets have lost the rhyme to pen a thought
A shared conversation is no longer heard
What once were is now no more
The fabrics that held us together
Like a favorite old flannel shirt
Has been substituted for blandness
Any trace of talent is shunned

Fox Tales

Replaced by three minute eggs
Which run at the sight of fresh blood?
Morality is yesterday's token
On a subway that has no local stops
All the landmarks that I once knew
Are merely distant places
Never to be visited again

East Coast Blues/ West Coast Clues

Left the city of Philly desperately needing a change of space
Touched down in the city by the bay dense fog shrouded the place
There was a pulsating urgency from the traffic and the hurried passersby
Checked in at the hotel Westin St. Francis at Union Square
The room overlooked an airshaft think The Getaway was filmed there
Purchased a ticket to board the trolley from Powell to Hyde
Up and down the steep hills of the city what a thrill of a ride
At Fisherman's Wharf where I savored the seafood and a song or two
Out in the bay is the rock Alcatraz silent as a tomb
Haunted by ghosts without a curfew
My instincts turned my direction in search of a particular bookstore
Called City Lights the Beat Generation poets called home but so much more
I passed a stone statue of St. Francis with, out stretched arms
Located in a parking lot beneath a tree of shady palms

Fox Tales

My path continued up Columbus through North Beach and Russian Hill
Where Joltin' Joe married Marilyn Monroe must have been a thrill
In front of St. Peter & Paul they were denied but took snapshots just the same
For they were divorced lived in sin but they knew how to play the game
The telephone and utility poles are painted in red white and green
Welcome to Frisco's Little Italy
Bistros line the sidewalks shimmer with sheen
Murals depicting jazz greats of decades gone past
Adorn triangle shaped corners as if tramp steamers lofty mast
I at last entered the famous bookstore and explored what was within
Where in the bowels of the basement was Dylan sporting a grin
Reaching out I picked up the book and held it in my hand
Had reservations to purchase it but returned it to the stand
However I did buy a book that caught my curious eye
Exited the establishment where directly across
The thoroughfare is the Hungry Eye
In the alley named for Jack Kerouac who wrote On The Road
If you haven't read it take the time I promise your mind won't explode
Took a double decker tour bus to take in the city sights
Went past Lombard the crooked street and Pacific Heights

James R. Fox

Entered the Presidio where Mr. Disney has a museum
Just outside the gates Bullitt was filmed starring Steve McQueen
Over the Golden Gate Bridge the wind was whipping a summertime chill
Stopped at Haight-Ashbury thought of Jimi, Janus,
The Grateful Dead an LSD pill
Then on a full day excursion tour of Monterey, Pebble Beach
And Carmel by the sea
Rows and rows of artichokes, strawberries and garlic
As far as the eye could see
Went in search of John Steinbeck along Cannery Row
To my dismay the sea otter was the rage the writer a no show
Arrived in Carmel found an empty bench
Outside Bruno's deli and had a bite to eat
When all of a sudden a stranger appeared and exclaimed
Sir you're sitting in my seat
Now what were the odds that I'd taken his place?
When he returned with his purchase a strange look on his face
He had Down syndrome and proceeded to state
Kind sir, kind madam would you like to hear a joke without malice or hate
For he held in his hands a stack of index cards written neatly in pen
An expression of his humorous side he must have stated again and again
On the trip back while aboard the bus
As the sun was fading fast like the rest of us

Fox Tales

Melodious music of Chet Baker filled the air an artist without a brush
Now back at home returned from the coast with memories to share
Long ago gone are the hippies the poets the flowers in your hair
But that's just the way it's supposed to be one day we'll all be there

Focus on the Moment

With all the attractions that occur throughout the day
It seems to me that we are allowing precious moments to slip away
As we surf the internet, we slowly spin a web of isolation
Oblivious to what matters most instead existing into a state of self-desolation
There are many distractions to befuddle the mind
What to leave in, what to leave out, who stays, who gets left behind
A single lie is similar to a lone wolf where there is one a pack will soon follow
Thus if at a loss for words, stay silent, better to be safe than sound hollow
The grains of sand that amass upon a deserted tropical isle
Viewed only with a spyglass that was once the property of a pirate with style
So take it all in, this exact moment this space this time
A winters chill, an embers glow precise as a poet's words of rhyme

If I Had a Dream

They gathered in the meadow and fields to pray
To listen to the words he had promised to say
Many traveled for miles carrying heavy loads
Children and pets in tow mothers and fathers navigating perilous roads
All were drawn to witness the Sermon on the Mount
To be baptized in the waters with his hands dipped in the holy fount
There was a sea of humanity as far as an eagle could fly
Just as the sunset a hush set in like a soothing lullaby
Then a voice was heard everyone looked toward the east
Could this be the second coming that was foretold to say the least?
Every knee was bent head was bowed as the clouds began to part
The faithful with rosaries prayed to Mother Mary with all their heart
All were kindred, by the spirit in body and soul
Sister to sister brother to brother the broken circle once again now whole
And so it was as in the beginning on the first page of the Holy Book
A dream to build upon, a wish a silent prayer is all that it took

O Say Can't You See

O say can't you see
What you're doing to our liberty
For your time is a coming, long overdue
Americans will vote you out then what will you do?
Sure as the autumn leaves begin to fall
You'll soon awaken to the buglers call
Because of your decisions the forecast isn't good
When was the last time you set foot in our neighborhood?
Homes for sale, foreclosures by the score
Companies bankrupt, workers unemployed out the door
Social security retirees denied a cost of living wage
But the politicians are deaf to their rage
After all the president promised a change
When he took office and swore to rearrange
The way Washington was ruled he'd turn it around
Instead he has run the economy into the ground
He who has never held down a job but knows what's best
Created a cabinet of lawyers, snakes, skunks and crooks
    from east to west
Signed into law stacks of pages unread but never you mind
For the government is just, fair, color blind and kind
If things don't go in favor of their way
They point and accuse we inherited this mess yesterday
But months have passed and they ran up the bill
Like a drunken sleazy politician on the prowl for a thrill

Fox Tales

Now the time is at hand without further delay
Tell all your neighbors and friends to send them away
Vote them out of office these talking heads in designer suit
Let them flip burgers, greet Walmart shoppers, who gives
    a hoot
Bring our troops home and build hospitals and schools
The real jobs that count by Americans with tools
It is up to you, for destiny is at hand
To restore America as it was, God blessed this land
Our children and their children deserve nothing more
To live in peace and one day put an end to war
So in a nutshell let freedom ring
A nation not divided but united of thee I sing

Snap My Fingers

If I could snap my fingers
Snap my fingers
Snap my fingers
And somehow return to yesterday
To a time or place of my youth
If I could somehow find the way
I'd be playing stickball
Hanging out with the gang
Trying to find an echo in the hall

If I could snap my fingers
Snap my fingers
Snap my fingers
I'd be California dreaming
As I take the subway downtown
To where everything had meaning
The nights would be white
The days would be black
There'd be poems inspired to write

If I could snap my fingers
Snap my fingers
Snap my fingers
Drop a coin into the jukebox for fun
Shooting pool at the arcade in the smoky haze
As the Ventures played Walk Don't Run

Fox Tales

The late bell would ring in high school
Students and teachers would dash to and fro
The king and queen were everybody's fool

If I could snap my fingers
Snap my fingers
Snap my fingers
I guess I'd probably just stay put
For we are who we are
And time is never on our side
For youth is the eternal driver so they say
Black and white fuzzy dice dangle from the rearview mirror
And Buddy Holly forever sings Not Fade Away

Meet Me at the Club Déja Vu

I just awoke from the craziest dream
I felt like Dorothy in Kansas caught up in a twister
The doors were shakin' the walls were quakin'
And I was too petrified to scream
Then it was over just as fast as it had parted
And where was I, why I really could not tell
When all of a sudden I heard someone yell
There you are, let's get the party started

Meet me at the Club Déja Vu
For a night of merriment and fun
Where everyone knows your name
Be there be prompt at our secret rendezvous

There was Minnie the Moocher and Mack the Knife
Hello Dolly was sippin' a dry martini at the bar
It was so surreal I was having the time of my life
Miss Ella was escorted by the Duke I observed from afar
There was Dizzy, blowin' on his upturned horn
While Django fingered the strings on a gypsy guitar
Billie Holiday began to croon A Star Is Born
Jack Kerouac just back from the road lit up a Cuban cigar

Meet me at the Club Déja Vu
For a night of merriment and fun

Fox Tales

Where everyone knows your name
Be there be prompt at our secret rendezvous

It was the best of times
And I had a front row seat
While Miles, Benny, Cab, Satchmo and Gene
Kept the rhythm of the jitterbug beat
I didn't want it to ever end
But I began to get restless
As the dream began to fade
To a place where the river would bend

Meet me at the Club Déja Vu
For a night of merriment and fun
Where everyone knows your name
Be there be prompt at our secret rendezvous

HALOS FOR BABIES

Who keeps you on your toes watches only cartoon shows?
Always up late at night has to go potty can't sleep without a light
Your house is constantly a mess, could use a break more or less
There are toys on the stairs, bubble gum stuck in their hair

Without a doubt they can drive you plumb crazy
Forever on the go, you're never lazy
No ifs no buts and no maybes
That's what God had in mind, halos for babies

Who needs a diaper changed as the pot overflows on the range?
You chauffeur them here and there, to the doctors or daycare
Take that out of your mouth or you'll choke
I'm too young for gray hair or a stroke
There are not enough hours in the day you can't wait to hit the hay

Without a doubt they can drive you plumb crazy
Forever on the go, you're never lazy
No ifs no buts and no maybes
That's what God had in mind, halos for babies

Fox Tales

When I was single I had the time of my life, full of vigor free from strife
Came and went where I may, made the most out of everyday
Never in my wildest dream I'd end up married
Have kids if you know what I mean
But it only goes to show, the baby has its toes
Stuck in the vacuum cleaners hose

Without a doubt they can drive you plumb crazy
Forever on the go you're never lazy
No ifs no buts and no maybes
That's what God had in mind, halos for babies

Hopalong, Gene & Roy

When I was a little boy, my greatest joy
Was playing cowboys with my six-shooter cap pistol toy
I wore a Silver Star, chaps, spurs at the make believe rodeo
The bad guys wore bandanas so their faces would not show

Yippee I A, Yippee I O
Davy Crockett with Jim Bowie at the Alamo
The Cisco Kid and Pancho in sombreros, boy oh boy
Tall in the saddle with Hopalong, Gene & Roy

Who could ever forget Jesse James and his brother Frank?
When they rode into town to rob the First National Bank
There was Doc Holliday and the Earp's holding guns in their hand
At the OK Corral a few paces away, the Clanton boys and their band

Yippee I A, Yippee I O
Davy Crockett with Jim Bowie at the Alamo
The Cisco Kid and Pancho in sombreros, boy oh boy
Tall in the saddle with Hopalong, Gene & Roy

A bullwhip would snap and crack, dressed all in black was Lash LaRue
Holding a dead man's hand of Aces and eights

Fox Tales

Wild Bill Hickok's days were through
The Lone Ranger on Silver and Tonto bareback riding Scout
Left behind a silver bullet, when they rode out of town, everyone would shout

Yippee I A, Yippee I O
Davy Crockett with Jim Bowie at the Alamo
The Cisco Kid and Pancho in sombreros, boy oh boy
Tall in the saddle with Hopalong, Gene & Roy

Now I'm an old grandpa, with grandkids on my lap
But every now and then I like to take a nap
Where do all the cowboys go after they all die?
Home on the range with ghost riders in the sky

Yippee I A, Yippee I O
Davy Crockett with Jim Bowie at the Alamo
The Cisco Kid and Pancho in sombreros, boy oh boy
Tall in the saddle with Hopalong, Gene & Roy

We're Not Heading Off to War Any More

The hour is upon us, we are at the brink of war
Can you tell us what the hell are we fighting for?
There are foreign ships anchored off our shores
Just waiting to unload their goods into all the stores
They make all the clothes toys and cars
Once the finest ever made were stamped with stars, red and white bars
Among us everywhere are homeless vets who can't find a home
Discarded, disabled, displaced, through the subways and alleys they roam
I'm tired of flag draped coffins holding only remains
When will we learn that nothing stays the same?
So tell me mister politician what have you got to say?
Go tell it on the mountain, bow your head and pray
For it is you who stir the pot, who stokes the flames ever so hot
And what have we got to show for it, look around not a lot
We have been to the four corners of the world to state our case
But look at our nation, a fragmented and disillusioned place
Spend trillions of dollars that were borrowed from China

Fox Tales

When the IOU comes due, we'll be destitute not finer
This land was your land, this land was my land
But now its owners have blood on their hand
Those in power who abuse, point fingers and accuse
Beware of patriots, for they are traitors who light the fuse
Generations come of age and duty calls
But when will common sense clog up the halls?
Will it take a declaration of separation to cease?
When America can once and for all have peace
Hear the voices in the streets, for they are the choir
Listen to the lowest of the low, instead of the higher
Now is the time, for the past shall never return
And tomorrow is a new sun that we may never earn
The zodiac is at the cusp, the stars all in align
The architect of all creation, the grand design
Knows that what began will soon come to pass
When all the sand will be at the bottom of the hourglass
Outside the Garden of Eden when Cain killed Abel
Wars have been fought over battlefields and at chess table
Perhaps one day there shall be a peaceful outcome
When all can rest their heads after day's work is done
It can be done it must be done, cast all differences aside
For what divides us can be bridged all of us must decide
So that once and for all the notion of war
Shall never be carried on incoming tides to our shore

What If Write Was Wrong?

With a cup of coffee and newspaper
Firmly seated at the breakfast table
I peruse the front page to the obituaries
As I read the words it occurred to me
If everything we were ever taught
Are merely folklore, myths or just a fable
Columbus sailed the ocean blue in 1492
But how do we know, there isn't any clue
The Pilgrims settled at Plymouth Rock
And partook in the first Thanksgiving
However the Indian tribes would surely debate
This tale was half-baked beans, served inside an earthen crock
The Civil War was fought by the North against the South
Doubt dare I say, West versus East by word of mouth?
At Ford's Theater with gun in hand, Booth shot Abe Lincoln
By all accounts he was captured in a warehouse, what was he thinkin'?
Among the famous of the missing are Amelia Earhart and Judge Crater
What if they opted out, to take a powder and see you all later?
In Dallas, Texas the president in a car without a roof
Oswald fired at JFK but did not die, for he was bulletproof

Fox Tales

An astronaut stepped foot onto the moon, for the world to see
Hollywood filmed it in vivid color no way you can fool me
What if E=mc2 was just a code, concocted by a janitor at MIT?
I could go on and on about quantum physics, theories of conspiracy
Where the truth may lie are between the words unexplainably
Cold case files locked away, hidden beneath a cloak of secrecy
Like ancient Egypt where the Pharaohs were entombed for eternity
Did Edgar Allan Poe really hear the raven tapping at his door?
Without Dr. Watson's assistance Sherlock Holmes hadn't a clue
Need I say more?
I can venture a guess and say matter of fact you think I've finally gone mad
But for every lunatic in the asylum, there resides a genius
Smug content and glad

In the Heart of the City

It is tough to survive on your own in the city
Where you are just another dreamer without pity
You stepped off a bus from the middle of nowhere
With a beaten up guitar case and a pocketful of carfare
Dreams of a stream of consciousness and fate
Had urged you to depart you couldn't wait
For like so many before that needed a change
You took that decisive step away from the range
Tacked a short note upon the front door
Written in pencil I'm leaving home tired of being poor
There has to be more to life than just this
I'm tired of star gazing it's time to follow my secret wish
Neon lights bleary eyes sawdust on the floor
An audition to showcase your style and a lot more
From the heart you sang an original ballad that you wrote
Cast aside the current trend who haven't an original note
Now not everyone will make the cut and survive
The odds are stacked against you to stay alive
It may take a lifetime of pounding and knocking on doors
Catching catnaps while on the road in between tours
Fame doesn't come cheap, for it comes with a price to pay
Either you accept the hand of fate, bite the bullet or pray
Secondhand stores that sold obscure record albums and rare books
Have been replaced by high-rise penthouse apartments owned by crooks

Fox Tales

Be careful not to let them invite you into their deadly corner
Many have tried, all have died, their fame faded left for the mourner

The Lady Will Always Be a Star

There once was a girl who sang and played the guitar
She was gifted and spread her wings to fly far
While others sought fortune and fame
The flowing hair lass had other plans on how to play the game
Bell-bottom jeans, day glow posters and tied dyed clothes
Concerts in the Village cafes at far and away shows
The message was always so refreshing like an early morning rain
As her fingers caressed the strings, her voice to entertain
She stayed true to her craft paying attention to detail
Unlike some lost & forgotten souls who sell their music below retail
Kept her focus on the moment and didn't fall into their trap
Like so many of her generation that grew old lost in the gap
Just by chance I jotted down her name that popped up in a book
I sent her a poem perchance with hopes she might look
And to my surprise soon thereafter I received a reply
The poem may have caused a spark, perhaps it captured her eye
Now we have never met face to face, I do not want to impose

Fox Tales

At this stage of my life I've slowed down more or less I suppose
From the kindness of her heart I received her latest CD
Who would have thought a celebrity would reach out to me?
Most only show up for the gig, play their tunes for the masses
Leave their fans out in the cold, while they hide behind dark tinted glasses
Fame & fortune are the twins that always arrive together
But not for the lady mentioned, she has only mellowed for the better
What has been accomplished will live on by other musicians that's for sure
For she will leave behind a lasting impression
A catalog that will forever endure

Trip to Ego

Convoluting weather ballooning, mystics in a row
Broke down and busted, nobody trusted, a one trick pony rodeo
Exodus out of Eden ticket punched, at the turnstile gate
Belly dancers in denial, a fortuitous date with fate
Multiplication, immigration, sincerity seals it all
Humanity, hypocrisy, remnants of a recent squall
Cascade rainbow above the palisades, atheists hike the Chisholm Trail
Literature, Daguerreotypes, votive candles in the mall
Hidden ancient codes, monoliths etched in stone
Pension checks, assembly line rejects, stereo in monotone
Druid priests, neckerchiefs, hobgoblin with leprechaun
Through the portals of the sublime, spun with skeins of yarn
Nothing matters, everything matters, abstract art of design
Ukulele-playing grifters Canary's in the mine
Veni, vidi, vici, pathos themed fiestas
Cucumber cactus salad, comedy and tragedy siestas
Existentialism, pomposity of degradation
A conundrum in flux, continuous desolation
Strings are always attached, fleeting moments never more
We are all but a last gasp away beware of a knock upon the door

That's Just the Way It Is

It's nobody's business but my own
What books I read or who I'm talkin' to on the phone
Seems to me that everybody's in your face
Who's tellin' who all over the place
I'd rather they all just disappear or jump in a well
They got their opinions & I got mine for a spell
Land mines are just waiting to take you out
Be careful where you tread I'm sure don't you doubt
Not everyone has your best intentions in mind so beware
I'd hate to tell the next of kin you're in intensive care
Turn on the news there's chaos in the streets
Just as plain as when you awake there's wrinkles in them sheets
Legend has it that Pandora had a golden box
As long as it was unopened all were safe for it contained a pox
Well curiosity killed more than a nine lives cat
And later than sooner we'll all be passin' the hat
With chisel in hand this cherished land is being dismantled brick by brick
This Promised Land torn asunder by holier than thou are making me sick
The orator is in denial for the sermon he'll never preach
For we are all sinners in the same sinking boat just out of reach

After All This Time

We shared an apartment in the city once, when we were young
But it wasn't meant to be, I was aloof and you were high strung
We used to frequent the park until it grew dark
And took in a foreign film or two just for a lark
Then came the fighting, the pills and the booze
You offered me an ultimatum, I couldn't refuse
I had inspiration's to write a bestseller book
You set your sights to sing your songs or to be a cook
We said our goodbyes on the brownstone stoop
Like two love birds we spread our wings we flew the coop
But that was so long ago when you headed west
I was determined to give it a go, I tried my best
We said our goodbyes on the old brownstone stoop
Like two love birds we spread our wings we flew the coop
But that was so long ago when you headed west
I was determined to give it a go, I tried my best
You suddenly came to mind after all these years
Through the many gin mill doors, shot of bourbon and beers
In the obituaries there were a few lines that said you had died
You had a long illness, fought the good fight, Lord knows you tried
Maybe if we stuck it out, maybe things could have been better

Fox Tales

I still remember your smell it lingers on the last letter
The one that you left on the kitchen table
Through bloodshot eyes I cried, my hands shook so unstable
Sometimes the best things come when we aren't ready
They are cast aside for now's not the time to be rock steady
The taxi's waiting I've got someplace to go
After all this time I love you more than you'll ever know

Who Am I To Judge?

Who am I to judge for I have never walked in your shoes?
Who among us hasn't acted foolish as if there was nothing to lose?
When things go so horribly wrong, it is then when we need help the most
In our hour of darkness we seek consolation yet we appear as a ghost
We get down on our knees and ask God for forgiveness
To help with the burden that is our personal business
It is all so easy to point fingers and accuse
But if it happens to you, what would be your excuse?
The world can be a wonderful place and also quite cold
Close friends can warm you like a fire, or shun you as you grow old
Deepest thoughts and decisions are strictly our own
To be judged one day after we have departed they will be known
A birth in a stable, fasting in the desert, turning water into wine
I'll help with your cross, if you help with mine

Gone Way Too Soon

They flipped a coin for the last airplane passenger seat
Because the tour bus was breaking down and had no heat
It started at Lubbock and crash landed in a field at Clear Lake
Buddy Holly had it all make no mistake
Well Alright, I'll Think It Over & Rave On
Still can't believe that he's checked out & unfortunately gone

She drove us all Crazy with that God gifted voice
No Cupie doll carnival consolation prize or cheesy second choice
I Fall To Pieces with Sweet Dreams (Of You)
Patsy Cline, take a bow your music will forever remain new
Hey Good Lookin', Move It On Over cause I Seen The Light

Just a good ol' boy too tired of hard livin'
Lost under his Stetson hidin' from sight
Died with his boots on at 29 in the backseat of a fancy car
Hank Williams flame went out like a shooting star

Buddy, Patsy & Hank we have you'll to thank
For supplying the gas to fill up the tank
Maybe Baby, She's Got You, In A Mansion On The Hill

Buddy, Patsy & Hank, Lord have mercy, you gave us many

Fox Tales

   a thrill
Your songs inspired us to make love underneath a full moon
You were just getting started, when you suddenly departed
Gone way too soon

Links of a Chain

We are all connected to one another
Grandmothers and Grandfathers
Mothers and Fathers
Husbands and Wives
Sons and Daughters
Brothers and Sisters
Aunts and Uncles
Nieces and Nephews
Cousins and Friends
Neighbors and Acquaintances
Strangers that we pass but never notice
With each birth a new link is formed
Likewise with death we lose another
Our chain can be as weak as gum wrappers crafted at camp
Or strong as an anchor chain that holds fast to the sea bottom
It is imperative to tell one another how important they are in our lives
For once they are gone it will be too late
And today's sunset eventually becomes tomorrow's sunrise
May the strongest link forever, remain anonymous?
So that the weakest will never feel alone or abandoned

Battered Guitar Case

I'm traveling somewhere on the road between Syracuse to Spokane
Aboard a Greyhound bus surrounded by strangers with no name
Seems like it's been ages ago when I was last home
Entertained in honkytonk's and where the winos often roam
Savored a slice of key lime pie at Key West on Mallory Square
Watched as the sun slowly set with a beach girl who had the fairest of hair
Arrived at the gates of Graceland to play for the King
But was notified sorry son but you aren't scheduled to sing
Time and again I often question myself for the choices I've made
Finished playing a gig, then having checks bounced after getting paid
I've slept on a hard bus depot bench
Stranded at Frostbite Falls deep in December
Worn out dozens of cowboy boots, second hand suits too many to remember
It's just me and my guitar inside this battered guitar case
Handed down from my grandpa with a deep wrinkled smile on his face
He said now sonny boy if you treat her well she'll be your best friend
Will never let you down be there for you time and again
It is a perfect fit any old guitar will do, just take your pick

Fox Tales

Practice every day change the strings take medicine when you're sick
There have been times when my key wouldn't open the lock
Had nowhere to turn, deciding whether to pawn or to hock
But I could never do that I'd be letting more than myself down
Grandpa has left a long time ago, buried on the outskirts of town
I may never see my name up in lights or on a billboard sign
As long as I have my battered guitar case I'll do just fine

Cervesa Tequila & Gin

It was south of the border in a Mexican cantina
When I stopped in for a drink
Buenos Diaz senor said the lovely senorita
As she smiled and gave me a wink
My name is Ester, are you here for the fiesta?
I replied no, I'm just taking it slow as I swiveled the barstool with my feet
The clock on the wall chimed for all, announcing the time of the day
When in through the doors came three hombres who shouted ole'
They held in their hands large acoustic guitars
Performers of a Mariachi band
To my surprise the sound of castanets joined in as Ester started to dance
The fandango her bare feet were amazing her face enhanced with romance
I couldn't take my eyes off her as she began to shimmy and shake
My hands were a trembling, the crescendo ascending
It felt like an earthquake
For the moment nothing else mattered even though I was hiding my fears
I've been on the run for stealing a sum and one day I'd be judged by my peers

Fox Tales

So I'm taking it slow, wherever I go, hoping they'll never show
The long arm of the law, always quick on the draw
After me for taking the dough
Through the swinging doors entered a desperado dressed all in black
Everyone feared him he was called El Diablo, but only behind his back
A wide brimmed sombrero in one hand a silver pistolero
The other held open a sack
He was here for the cash then a quick getaway and then be gone in a flash
Now although I'm a thief, it is my belief that you never steal from the poor
So I turned around and without making a sound
Stood blocking the cantina door
He poked the sombrero with the edge of his pistolero
And said what have we here?
A gringo who defies me do you want to die today
Then get on your knees and pray
While he turned his full attention to me, Ester along with the band
Assailed him with bottles, elbows and kneecaps, anything near at hand
Though he was tough it soon got rough
He shouted Santa Maria I've had enough
We all cheered as he slowly crawled out to his horse
Mounted up and rode out of town
Drinks on the house, we are rid of the louse, the gringo has saved the day

James R. Fox

From net zero I felt like a hero, my past a Roulette's wheel
    spin to win
Now I'm sharing the booty with my Mexican cutie
Drinking cervesa tequila and gin

CROSS WITH ME

Can you help me cross over to the other side?
For the river is very deep, the river very wide
Help me dear Jesus, take hold of my hand
Calm the waters erase my fears, let me understand
That what is to be found, on the outer bank?
Is worth the struggle, I have you to thank
I am a sinner so I know there is a price to pay
So it is told Michael had a boat to row ashore
I only possess this broken in two weather beaten oar
There is a ferryman I hear tell, who carries passengers across the river Styx
But I know he can't be trusted, I won't be fooled I'm onto his tricks
He tells all who will listen to climb aboard there is no toll
After the ferry departs you can never disembark, without giving up your soul
So here I now stand at the edge of the rivers bank
If I can only cross over to the far side, I'll have you to thank

My Very Own Bucket List

Some folks I know are content to stay
In their rocking chairs and fritter the day away
Or else feel sorry for themselves woe is me
But that's not for me I'd rather be busy as a bee
Now at this moment in my life as the hours grow short
I've always wanted to do creative things like sailing port to port
Or being aboard a circus rain among the clowns in the caboose
Hosing down the pachyderms, feeding the dromedaries, loose as a goose
Add to my, to do list a scuba dive beneath a crystal clear sea
Exploring a coral reef, a sunken pirate ship, oh glory me
Don't keep all of your wishes bottled up inside
Where they'll never escape because of doubt, unable to decide
Growing old isn't for sissies, it takes fortitude and wit
It can't be taught you can only earn it, bit by bit
Wouldn't you rather have a smile on your face?
As you exit the plane skydiving into open space
Than lying in a nursing home all alone on your own
Where strangers check on you, like an orphan without a home
I know that my odds are slim, that I may never win, but that's okay by me

Fox Tales

For if we never strive to keep dreams alive then it really wasn't meant to be
I've been lucky so far, better off than most I must confess
How many are in dire straits more or less I can only venture to guess

Make Mine to Go

It was the start of a new day so why the delay waiting on a cup of joe
When I got to the counter I checked my watch and said
Make it a regular to go
As I headed on out I noticed what appeared to be a pile of rags
But upon further inspection there stirred a life beneath tattered flags
I noticed a patch on the left shoulder of the 101st Airborne
A Screaming Eagle a fellow paratrooper now just someone to scorn
I extended my hand then bent down to meet him face to face
He sadly smiled with a hypnotic look like he was in some far off place
I'm a vet just like you though I bet you've had it tough
Nope he just stated I got no medals, ribbons or other heroic stuff
It's my fault you see, blew it all I lost my home and family
To my demons of drugs and gambling, acting selfishly
Got nobody to blame so here I am playing the cards I was dealt
I got a lump in my throat as I opened the cup and took a coffee belt
Is there anything I can do, for you don't belong out on the street?
I'll be okay been here since yesterday taken a load off my sore feet

Fox Tales

It then occurred to me that I was running late as I began to turn away
But something was tugging at me that I could not see imploring me to stay
With tears in my eyes I tried not to cry, but the stranger felt my pain
I see you've got troubles too, was it a venture all in vain?
His words hit me like an IED while on tour in Afghanistan
The Humvee was blown to bits, but I escaped the solitary man
He exclaimed I can tell that you've been there and back through hell
Only a vet would know ones fate that fought the enemy and lived to tell
We can wave the flag, cheer for the country
But forget about the veteran's woes
But remember this, if not for them who would protect us from our foes?
I'll never forget that fateful day when I met one of the brave
How many are but a mere last breath away from being unable to save
It's up to you and you and you to do the best to help your fellow man
For no matter where you hail from, city, town or state we are all American

CHAPTER & VERSE

A twister is a comin'/ a twister is a comin'
It's headin straight toward town
A twister is a comin'/ a twister is a comin'
It will leave everything in its path upside down

The rivers are a risin'/ the rivers are a risin'
Like Noah & his Ark during the Great Flood
The rivers are a risin'/ the rivers are a risin'
The lands a hemorrhaging veins of blood

Wildfires are a blazin'/ wildfires are a blazin'
Are we so blind that we cannot see?
Wildfires are a blazin'/ wildfires are a blazin'
Mother Nature is thinning out the herd unconditionally

Head for higher ground/ head for higher ground
The Four Horsemen of the Apocalypse are heading your way
Head for higher ground/ head for higher ground
For what we reap is what we sow & now is the time to pay

From Here to There

Toe-stompin' hillbilly's deep in Cajun country home of the bayous
Whittle away their lives outfitted in bib overalls and go without shoes
But ask any local who can play the best jug band music ever heard
Snakes alive shake a beehive wrestle a gator, all so absurd
These good ol' boys have a knack to fiddle play and strum a banjo
Conjure up Mark Twain piloting a paddle wheeler down the Ohio
Like none I've ever seen before, richer than Jethro T's bodacious turpentine
That passes for homegrown moonshine, better than imported fancy wine
Mosquitoes bigger than your fist will bite at you for a snack
You could swat your life away, at the nine to five job
Then croak from a heart attack
On the front porch of Goober's General Store kids, doin' the hand jive
Slappin' their hands every which a way keepin' the beat alive
Earn their keep the only way they know, passin' around the proverbial hat
A gumbo of nationalities, who were never welcomed here, imagine that

Fox Tales

From deep in the woods to the local neighborhood
Snappin' fingers on the stoop
Under the boardwalk making out, up on the roof, pigeons in the coop
Doo wop, folk, a little of this, a lot of that, a dash of gospel with soul
Country, fill in the blanks, jazz, blues, it's all rock & roll
The beat will always go on long after the greats have left the stage
Music & lyrics forever joined, black & white upon the page

Have You Got Something to Say?

I can't recall the actual time of day
But it occurred in the month of May
We had just moved from one garage to another
When I was approached by a union member
In regards to raising the red white and blue
I was soon called on the spot that I felt was long overdue
From a creased up piece of paper I recited my thoughts and read
How I felt about Memorial Day what popped into my head
After I was done there was a round of applause from almost everyone
It took me aback I must admit, not one to stand out, glad that it was done
Then as I began to walk away a coworker suggested, why not write a book?
What was it that I said, a few sentences that I read, as bait on a hook?
So I took the dare the challenge to heart
But where to begin, how does one start?
I had an idea or so I thought, about nothing serious, just for fun
And so I started chapter one, easier said than done
What I thought would be a tale of friends and family
Soon turned onto a much different path, a deep mystery

Fox Tales

Two priests, one professor oh and the devil of many faces
I had opened a door and in stepped characters, from different places
The story was drawing me in, as if I was supposed to tell
Of good bad and indifferent, angels and demons heaven and hell
Thus the Map of the Carpenter came to fruition
Drawn from an admirer who had intuition
However I was urged to continue, for the ending had to say more
So back to the table I was lucky and able to whet and to core
A sequel titled Christmas Eve
Now I was content to leave
But a hunger still persisted and no matter how I resisted
I resumed the tale thus again, with new characters that assisted
For it was only fitting to conclude as a trilogy Wisdom of Wishes
How did Jesus feed the masses with just five bushes of loaves and fishes?
Everyone has a story to tell, but the odds to succeed one can never tell
I'll still dream away and maybe one day my words will ring true as a bell

Now It's Too Late to Say Goodbye

Yesterday's gone we can't bring it back for it has set sail
Like the assorted bills, catalogs, your postcard in the mail
That showed a cute cottage nestled beside a mountain lake
We once had it all, where did we go wrong, where was the mistake?

Words are all we have after all this time
It was never what is yours is also mine
One of us stayed while the other left now I know why
Now it's too late to say goodbye

Today I am left with empty promises that cover the floor
We broke each other's heart need I say more?
Dreams of a lifetime together filled with romance and fun
Now dark clouds have filled my sky where there should be sun

Words are all we have after all this time
It was never what is yours is also mine
One of us stayed while the other left now I know why
Now it's too late to say goodbye

Tomorrow may never come perhaps today will be my last
Just as the youngest become the oldest nothing is built to last

Fox Tales

As I lock the door, turn off the light it was never meant to
    be
I wish you well, may your dreams come true, c'est la vie

Words are all we have after all this time
It was never what is yours is also mine
One of us stayed while the other left now I know why
Now it's too late to say goodbye

Recalibrating

My life has been a mess these past few days
I need to reassess get my head above this cloudy haze
It feels like I'm stuck going up a hill in the wrong gear
Wearing my heart on my sleeve, crying in my beer

The internal compass needs recalibrating my very own GPS
I've been coasting on autopilot for so long, more or less
Time to dust off the old guitar I've got songs to play
Get busy with life, don't stew and wither away

Have to find the time to teach children the ABC's
Thank the Lord for all the He has given, on my bended knees
Provide comfort and hope to those that mourn
A sanctuary, a safe haven, shelter from the storm

Been tossed about stem to stern in raging seas
Cancer has that effect on all, not just who has the disease
What awaits us all on the other side, no one can tell
Who hasn't tossed a coin over their shoulder into a wishing well?

The play, the act, the scene, mere words upon the page
The actors roles constantly change, who is the hero, villain, fool, the sage
Yes it's true we have played them all every now and then

Fox Tales

Round and round the carousel goes, we get on and off time and again

Stillness

As a photograph forever captures the scene
As a thought later on instills a dream
When a spider opts to spin its web upon a wheel
When a child looks for comfort that only you can feel
The frost upon a verdant field of which show no evidence of life
The silence within shadows ever present between husband and wife
Haunting melodies of walks upon cobblestones underfoot
Hallucinations induced by a cupful of rosemary, honey, ginger root
Kindness rarely ever pays a visit to the poor
Keeping the needs of the squeaky heels their wants ever more
But who shall open the doors to the barn
Baling the hay, protecting the herd from any harm
Cast your hopes, your fears in a faded worn pocket
Cherish your lost loved ones heart inside a silver locket

The Invisible Man

I am a man who you'll never meet
I walk the streets alone sad and incomplete
We were to be married one fine day in September
Forever as husband and wife, don't you remember?
But then he came along and stole your heart
What was I to do, after you said goodbye, I fell apart

I am the invisible man
Doing the best that I can
I will forever be on the move and endlessly roam
For I have no address, a place that I can call home

Who was there for you, when the chips were down?
Who cheered you up, made you happy, a smile in place of a frown
You and I had it all, a special chemistry
But I was so wrong, it just wasn't meant to be

I am the invisible man
Doing the best that I can
I will forever be on the move and endlessly roam
For I have no address, a place that I can call home

I pass by the restaurant where we used to wine and dine
At our favorite table near the window, how your eyes would shine

Fox Tales

All the guys would take a quick passing glance
Everyone could tell, we were captivated in our romance

I am the invisible man
Doing the best that I can
I will forever be on the move and endlessly roam
For I have no address, a place that I can call home

I will never get over you
Maybe someday, after all we went through
Are these tears in my eyes, or just drops of rain
It really doesn't matter, for there is no way to take away the pain

I am the invisible man
Doing the best that I can
I will forever be on the move and endlessly roam
For I have no address, a place that I can call home

MYTHS & LEGENDS

A manuscript on a roll of teletype that spans more than two hundred feet
A concrete highway from east to west
Where the sun and the moon shall never meet
A bodega which never closes, that caters to inner city ethnic foods
A maximum security prison that is home to a lifetime of moods
Behind the stage curtain, nerves a jitter with a final microphone check
Before the singer slings the guitar and adjusts the harmonica around his neck
When the teens turn into twenties without a single word to say
When the past has faded for the present and we are now old and gray
For the planets are in align, a spectacular zodiac design
Far from our eyes, light years away, a parallax paradigm
Our senses are numb, sublimely immune to the news
Omens proclaimed by oracles, surreptitious point of views
Film in high definition 3D to excite the audience with gasps of fright
Flashlights split the darkness, shine on clues hidden from sight

Key West

What is it about the island that attracts me so?
Maybe if I were a seafarer from long ago
It would make common sense to me
But one too many hurricanes will do tricks on you, not just at sea
However, it is more than that, yet I cannot really describe
This feeling, a sense of belonging, pulsating deep inside
From the first moment I set foot on this paradise isle
I didn't want to leave, I could sense God's smile
Try as I may to put into words, for someone who has never been there
Is like believing in ghosts, truth be told, they are everywhere
Roosters, chickens cross the roads, geckos check into your room for fun
Bicycles, trolleys, conch trains, mopeds, taxis, pedestrians under a setting sun
Duval Street, Mallory Square, music, food, artisans and such
Savior all that it has to give, slow down and take the time, no need to rush
For all the many that I have encountered and listened to what I had to say
That I am an author, wrote about the island and the famous Hemingway
The doors to the church were open, allowing me to truly be myself

Fox Tales

I hoisted the sails yes indeed, like a favorite book you took
    me off the shelf
I shall forever have the yearning to return again one day
To eventually reside in Key West and never go away
For if there truly exists a heaven right here on earth
It is on this tiny dot of land, rare as doubloons
Pieces of eight a pirate's booty of worth

The Old Man

There's an old man out on the porch sitting in a rocking chair
His hair is white a page of the good book is open but all he does is stare
The wind is shifting turning the sky a deep dark gray
A storm is a brewing churning like a locomotive comin' this a way
But the old man doesn't flinch, just rocks the old bones to & fro
His memory pulls him back to when he was a kid so many summers ago
When he & old Buck would skip stones & fish down at the creek
After sneaking out from the Bible school meeting, meant for the meek
Yup, just him & old Buck one kid black, the other kid white
They never could see color, both bled red
Knew what was wrong, as well as right
Closer than brothers, sensed their every thoughts before words were spoken
Back then it was a different time, livin' in the South
All was fine, nothing was broken
That was the picture for the outsiders to see, for they wanted to be left alone
Don't go snoopin' or lookin' for trouble
Stirrin' up a hornet's nest, bad to the bone

Fox Tales

Then came the Freedom Riders followed by horsemen
With torches and white sheets
We'll teach them all a lesson they'll never soon forget, we own these streets
For I ask, wasn't this the reason why the Civil War was fought?
Gettysburg is the resting place of many blue & gray, or so we were taught
But it seems that it comes down to one or the other, as jam and bread
Such as a page of white needs ink of black in order to be read
Or a corncob pipe is of no use, unless it's broken in just right
The old man closes his eyes for the last time, out went the light

I Had No Choice But to Leave

If you are reading this letter, I hope you're feeling better, it pains me to grieve
Say hello to aunt Flo, also uncle Joe righteous
Kinfolk without bias who believe
Like a black cat who crossed your path, late one autumn moonless night
If not for your curiosity, determined to investigate
Turning on the front porch light
As we met face to face I was trying to erase the past, ready set to explode
Hunted by the law, felt like Robert Mitchum fleeing down Thunder Road
I was on the lam after pulling off a bank heist, that's not who I am
Fell into the laps of some unsavory saps, a fine pickle of a jam
So now I'm out on Highway #1 not resting until day is done
Hope to relax on some deserted beach get tanned as a raisin in the sun
Now don't get sad & blue everything I told you, facts were not true
Oh maybe let's forget, it's better left unsaid, I could never ever hurt you
But I've got to follow my dreams up or down these turbulent rapid streams

Fox Tales

For what good is chasing windmills, or living on the edge
 of extremes
May you always cast a glow wherever you go
Forever in your debt, you took me in
Was desperate, bruised, tattered, lost, filled to the brim
 with many a sin
Habits of mine tend to unwind weave a silken web of
 suspicion & mystery
Therefore I'll be just a faded memory
A journey of burning bridges ancient history

Houston We Have a Problem

Houston we have a problem, but not in outer space
It's closer to home where the longhorns roam, wildfires all over the place
If you ever set foot in Texas, then you have sand in your boots
At San Antone where Crockett & Bowie fought
For the republic, planted the roots
An assorted collection of ragtag volunteers a bunch aptly called Texicans
Against all odds, faced Santa Ana's army thousands of Mexicans
Colonel Travis with sword in hand drew a line in the sand
Remember the Alamo for this is our final stand
Inside the Hotel California, you can check in but never check out
The manager knows all the guests on a first name basis, this I have no doubt
Every evening he entertains hosting lavish parties, enjoys the finest of wine
Never chilled always Luke warm, laced with just a hint of turpentine
Oh, I know who the culprit is, that started these wildfires
Uses the seven deadly sins as kindling, evil motives are his desires
Now he is getting in his last licks and kicks out on old Route 66

Fox Tales

It's time to pack up his belongings and ship them back across the river Styx
The West coast has its share of earthquakes
The East coast has its full of snowflakes
The great Lone Star State has been parched dry, felt by every soul
Not seen the likes of this, since Woody Guthrie
Sang about the Oklahoma dust bowl
Some say it's our fault for abusing the land and never giving back in return
Waterfront property, golf courses to excess, when will we ever learn?
Building homes where before there were none
Cut down forests that provide shade from the sun
Yes Houston, we have a problem, but not in outer space
Respect Mother Nature or else they'll be no human race
I stood next to a biker looking at the sky
Colors of the rainbow shaped like a ball
We were amazed at the sight as the day turned into night
A moment shared that's all
Shook hands, smiled at each other, never got his name, felt two drops of rain
After all we are just ashes to ashes
Once we are gone that's all that shall remain

For Now Is the Time Not Tomorrow

Have you noticed what's happening throughout the land?
The young and the old are complaining they can't understand
How the bureaucrats, the bankers are a bunch of crooks
Spent all of our money, then cooked all the books
The time is way past, there's no room for more sorrow
For now is the time not tomorrow

In the garden Judas betrayed Jesus with a fatal kiss
Pilate washed his hands and proclaimed I'll have none of this
Living high in the sky, the fat cats in their corporate ivory tower
Better take notice for those in the streets will soon have the power
The time is way past there's no room for more sorrow
For now is the time not tomorrow

Gone are our homes, our jobs and our pride
We were all sold a bad bill of goods, without God on our side
Spent billions of bucks to explore outer space
While veterans returned missing limbs, lost and displaced

Fox Tales

The time is way past, there's no room for more sorrow
For now is the time not tomorrow

So look whose protesting, kids, union workers, dear ma and pa
Letting their voices be heard, coast to coast near and far
It's too late for promises, for too long we've been played for a fool
We want what's rightfully ours, not 40 acres and a mule
The time is way past, there's no room for more sorrow
For now is the time not tomorrow

A change is a coming, has been a long time brewing
People are edgy, tired of politics, the games, same old pot stewing
The Liberty Bell is cracked Lady Liberty has lost her crown
The Twin Towers are gone Wall Street players have corrupted the town
The time is way past, there's no room for tomorrow
For now is the time not tomorrow

There are no blue or red states, only a nation of confusion
Run by millionaires who should be placed in an institution
Please heed the call before it's too late
Then who'll be to blame with nothing left on an empty plate
The time is way past, there's no room for more sorrow
For now is he time not tomorrow

On the Road to Calvary

I set out to find the Garden of Eden
But I could not enter
For there were locks and chains at the gates
I searched high and low for unresolved questions
Answers never received from the thinkers, the poets, the greats
Contrary to public opinion, all roads do not lead to Rome
They all end at just one place, our final destination
It could be a lonely winding path
Or uneven filled with cracks and stone
We have no sense of direction
Left on our own, maybe close or far from home
If we are fortunate a Good Samaritan
Will help with our cross and lighten the load
Some will mock and jeer us for who we are
At times we are in the spotlight
But most of us will never shine
The play, the seasons, the joys and the sorrows
Our very own hourglass and how we use the time
From the moment we are born
To when we are called to go
It is the space in between that is granted
Fools waste it, while others share it
When it shall end, one never knows
Be kind to one another not just every now and then

Fox Tales

So finish what you have started
For the chance may never come again

The Invitation

I received an invitation in the mail just the other day
That my services are requested and to RSVP without delay
A reunion is the occasion black tie and tails would be the dress
Where do I begin, I need new clothes, I've aged, my hair is gray, I look a mess
It seems like ages ago since I was in demand
All those sleepless nights out on the road, playing in the band
I'd have to get new strings, tune up the old guitar
But who am I kidding arthritic fingers will get you only so far
But maybe I can fake it for a song or maybe two
Hey maybe I'll be better than you know who
The ones who thought they were king and queen remember when
And the rest of us were props if you know what I mean, no not again
You can't turn back the hands of time but wouldn't that be cool
I've seen enough of the old acts dying, to be young playing the fool
What to do, what to do, say yes or say no
I'm really flattered to be asked to the show
Who knows maybe I'll be requested to play the song I wrote

Fox Tales

On a scrap of motel stationary and postcards every word every note
It still haunts me the drugs the booze the ugly news
We had it all who didn't want to be in our shoes
But it all ended in a crash no more contracts no more deals
Out on the skids, barely getting by, existing on happy meals
From living the high life you know, the whole nine yards
Lost it all in a flash tumbling down like a house of cards
But I survived where others may God let them rest in peace
I miss them ever so, the good the bad to say the least
So here I am holding in my hands a tempting invitation
To RSVP what shall be my decision of perhaps reconciliation
They'll all stop and stare when I dazzle them with my flair
When I arrive hold the applause at the big affair
To be dressed up at long last somewhere to go
I'll turn all their heads, for I'll be the star of the rock & roll rodeo

The Last Kiss

Here is the love story about Flo and Joe
A couple of childhood sweethearts like Juliette and Romeo
They lived in a small town on the banks of the Kokimo
It was the winter of 1957 Joe was drafted and had to go

They were seniors went to the prom at Taft high school
Joe wore a sharkskin suit blue suede shoes he was Mr. Cool
Flo had on a pink fuzzy sweater a poodle skirt she was nobody's fool
All the kids went wild when the band started to play Don't Be Cruel

Joe worked after school to buy a two toned little Rambler Nash
He loved that car proud as a riverboat gambler paid in full with cash
So there was Flo and Joe inside the car with only the lights of the dash
The windows were all fogged up the brake was off they never felt the crash

When they didn't return home the very next day
Their families were worried where could they be God let us pray
The chief of police went to lover's lane out on the old highway

Fox Tales

Just the rear of the car could be seen frozen in the rivers ice far away

They held the funeral open caskets for all to view
So many attended Joe laid out in black Flo in a dress of blue
Was the chain of events that transpired just hearsay or really true
Young and in love were Flo and Joe so evident everyone knew

The tragic tale of Flo and Joe didn't end that fateful night
Nope some folks say they hear music and see a cars dome light
For on the anniversary of their death to set things right
Two silhouettes appear inside a heart sharing a kiss their last delight

FAITH

Let us give the devil his due
For he has been here since day one
While the rest of us
Are just passing through
There are sinners who do not hate all saints
And some saints do not hate all sinners
Does one really care?
If there are happy losers or sore winners
For only fools dress up in masquerade
But the wise can plainly see
Through their thinly
Disguised charade
Some believe that the Bible
Written by Matthew Mark Luke and John
Are nothing more than fairytales
A tapestry woven as a never ending fabricated yarn
What man was Jesus?
Who walked on water?
Raised the dead
Healed the sick
Turned water into wine
Only God can perform miracles
Not a man who claimed
To be divine
This is where faith steps in
To guide us along the way

Fox Tales

Why we bless ourselves
Get on our knees
With rosaries in hand then pray
Everything we are
From our head to our toes
Was created out of love
This precious gift called life
Where we have come from
To where we are destined to go
Is truly a mystery
That God only knows

Navy Blues

The pea coat I no longer possess
Along with the 13 buttons bell bottom blues
Left behind a long time ago
When I wore a younger man's shoes
I traveled light the world was my delight
Visited many a port here and there
Drunk like a skunk awoke in my bunk
Still smelling of stale beer and cigarettes
My head was pounding a sea bag full of regrets
A lifetime of being out at sea
But it wasn't meant to be
I miss the water, the rhythm of the swells
The time adrift the solitude that dwells
A mariner is meant to return
From the churning unknown
Yearning to feel the shore
Underfoot beaten torn and blown
Tattoo parlors, neon signs rusted cars beside the road
Handout bills, dark alley thrills
Shoulder a heavy load
Long-range weather forecast, a crystal shot glass
Try your hardest to make it last
Conquistadors, fatally gored matadors
A fortnight before the mast
Buff and spit shine polished cordovan dress shoes
Listening to the lonesome honky tonk blues

All for the Love of a Queen

My main squeeze is gone, checked out, she had her ticket punched for a destination unknown. I never saw it comin', although I should have been paying attention. I was sucker punched. So here's a tip for all you palookas out there, yeah I'm talkin' to you the brawlers who got their bells rung inside the ring way too many rounds ago. I've been on the canvas with a referee startin' to count me out, my manager chompin' on a stogie, the corner man just waitin' to throw in the towel, my eyes full of blood. I felt as if I was lookin' through stained glass windows of a church as a priest is about to give me last rites. Somehow I get to my feet, hands taped tight inside the gloves, grope for the ropes to help me from fallin' over on my mug. The ref wipes the sweat from the leather on the front of his shirt, asks me what round is it. I take a wild guess. He steps aside and here comes my worst nightmare. I'm fightin' for my life the challenger half my age, could be my kid if I ever managed to have one, not in this lifetime. Combinations tag me in the ribs and kidneys, sounds in my ears are muffled. Uppercuts to my jaw, the neck snaps back like a mattress coil. But I keep on goin' I got no choice. Finally the bell rings I stagger to my corner collapse exhausted on the stool the cut man goes to work applying pressure to staunch the nasty open wounds. Cold water is poured over my head and then down the front of

Fox Tales

my trunks, I grab a quick drink from the water bottle as the bell sounds. Somehow I manage to finish the bout the challenger wins. Not a happy ending just like in life stuff happens, deal with it. After the manager and the handlers get their cut of the purse I'm left with the rest. I look like I was in a head on collusion of a car wreck and I went through the windshield. I got just enough dough to get me home. When yours truly and the main squeeze first set up house we agreed to pool our savings. I found an old cigar box she put her loose change in it from her pocketbook and I did my fair share depositin' empty promises and a stack of IOU's. So here's the thing, a tip from a once has been contender. Be good to the one who loves ya who's always in your corner no matter what, all the little things mean the most. Don't sweat it because life is just a game, a shell game where you are tryin' to find the pea, or three card Monte a Jack, a Queen & a King. Pay close attention to the Queen but never lose sight of the Jack for he is the knave who will steal her away from the King.

Stewed, Screwed & Tattooed

Down at the local saloon, two fools sittin' on bar stools drownin' their troubles away. Said the old to the new "ya know what's the trouble with our youth, they can't handle the truth, full of malarkey, blue skies are always dark, feelin' sorry for themselves, a sorry lot a bunch of cryin' babies." Replied the new to the old "aren't you real bold, your generation who sold, took the money and ran, left us with nothin' but just grains of sand." The barkeep could almost smell that the outcome to all of this wouldn't end well. So he offered a refill on the house. "You see these hands sonny boy? They have dirt and grit under the nails, dug ditches and hammered the rails. I paid my dues for where I sit, proud to say my generation never quit." The new now quite irritated, "well good for you I'll keep my hands clean, make tons of money when I get my degree. I'll be free as a bird and king of the world." The barkeep just shook his head taking in all that was just said. "All brains, no guts, no glory seems to me it's everyone's story these days. Do you think I just walked into this bar and the previous owner just flipped me the keys and said 'so long take care you'll go far.' Hell no, I got debt up to my ears, the taxes are in arrears, plus the neighborhoods changin' hell yeah, I got plenty to fear." Then came the lull in the conversation, happens all the time at weddings, funerals any old usual occasion. As long as there are cards at the table, while the whiskey flows free and horses kick their heels inside the stable, they'll always be a changin' of the guard, sometimes change can be hard. Once long ago in the tiny town of Bethlehem, steel was king, locomotives, ships, skyscrapers soared, we had everything. Now freight trains are covered with graffiti, not used much these days, like before, when all you had to do was hop on board and explore. Bethlehem has a new casino now known as the Sands. A new steal city, it is such a pity. So as the shadows slowly creep in, the clock on the wall chimes for all. The barkeep exclaims "last call for alcohol." The two fools sip their last drying drip, toast one another for luck then settle up their tab walk arm and arm out the door. "See ya tomorrow, same time. I got your back, just as certain you got mine."

By His Hands We Are All Fed

I have an old black & white photograph of my maternal grandparents that is on the top of my dresser. They are dressed for a cold day, both of them are wearing heavy coats, a fedora is cocked slightly to the side on my grandfather's head. They are on the roof of a New York tenement where most of the working class lived back in the 30's & 40's. Their generation made do with the basic necessities. A cold beer a 5 cent cigar a new pair of nylons perhaps some flowers or a box of candy was a treat. A day at the beach was the closest thing to heaven they never complained or blamed anyone they lived paycheck to paycheck. They would be lost in the present day world of the haves and the have not's.

On my patio there is a sculpture of two hands together palms open with a small bird resting on the right hand. I fill it with water for the birds. I also fill the bird feeder which is a mixture of seeds and kernels of corn. The sparrows are able to eat from the feeder they push the larger seeds to the ground where the doves, ravens and an occasional squirrel or rabbit will partake of the food to keep them nourished and fed.

While the wealthy continue to shell out exorbitant amounts to rub shoulders with the movers and shakers, America's hungry wait on lines for a hot meal. After all the lavish dinners are done one can only ask, where are the leftovers and who will benefit from the table scraps? Surely the rich are never photographed leaving an event with a doggy bag in their possession.

If the animals can share the crops that were harvested in an orderly fashion, then why can't we? If every house of worship had a food pantry, if every sporting event, concert, museum or entertainment venue collected just one dollar for every ticket sold that went directly to the hungry we could aid assistance to our fellow neighbors from being hungry.

I do not have a Twitter, Hashtag account nor do I partake in Facebook or text. I'd rather speak to someone face to face but there are those who I have never met but I feel that we share common beliefs and helping those less fortunate. So if you feel inclined I would be grateful if you decide to pass this along. For by His hands we are all fed.

Shelter After the Storm

There was a concert at the Garden for the victims of Sandy
The hurricane not the beloved pooch of Little Orphan Annie
All the rockers & rollers showed up including Sir Paul
They played their decade's old tunes sung by one and all
As the large jumbo screens displayed tragic scenes of the crime
An outpouring of love from strangers donating their support and time
I hope they raised piles of money that goes to all in need
Not to a board of directors with their hands out in greed
Soon after the storm politicians all came by
Promising those affected not to leave them high and dry
Yet here it is as the last days of the year draw to a close
Families are displaced homes washed away and so it goes
I find it ironic that when other countries are in trouble
We answer the call send in the troops on the double
As the nation slowly approaches the fiscal cliff
Washington bigwigs won't budge scaring us all stiff
Before our taxes are raised let this set the tone
Stop all the foreign aid and bring the military home
Just think of all the jobs that could be made
Rebuilding the country an honest day's work plus getting paid
There will always be anarchist's atheist's assassin's thieves and crooks

Fox Tales

Sinners with halos angels among us how novel not printed
    in books
For Jesus had Judas among the twelve he trusted the most
But he was given to his accusers tortured pillar to post
Jesus fed the masses with two loaves of bread and five fish
This should be on everyone's Christmas wish list
We are all affected with the tides ebb and flow
Consider yourself blessed if you have someplace safe to go

A Fedora, an Echo and Shades

I had a dream last night
That took me back to long ago
To when I was a kid playing stickball
Johnny Ride the Pony and Ringalevio

Show me your cards and I'll show you mine
That's a good hand all aces and spades
What have I got you ask?
A fedora an echo and shades

We used to play board games
Monopoly Clue and often time's charades
As the hi-fi played our favorites
 Fond memories of watching the parades

Show me your cards and I'll show you mine
That's a good hand all aces and spades
What have I got you ask?
A fedora an echo and shades

Long before there was stereo and FM
Our transistor radio stations only had AM
But we'd listen until the batteries died out
To the oldies but goodies time and again

Fox Tales

Show me your cards and I'll show you mine
That's a good hand all aces and spades
What have I got you ask?
A fedora an echo and shades

It was a time of innocence
Where everyone got along
When your word was all that mattered
And friendship was our silver platter

Show me your cards and I'll show you mine
That's a good hand all aces and spades
What do I have you ask?
A fedora an echo and shades

But then like all dreams it slowly faded away
And I awoke to a world so different from the past
Like all good things
They aren't supposed to last

Show me your cards and I'll show you mine
That's a good hand all aces and spades
What have I got you ask?
A fedora an echo and shades

Scratch Off Fever Plans

If I were ever to hit the jackpot
I'd leave my car in the long-term parking lot
I'd pack for warmer weather yes indeed
And donate all of my possessions to those in need
Purchase a one-way ticket to some secluded tropical isle
Where I would live out the rest of my life in style
Feelin' the sand slide between my toes
All decked out in tank tops flip-flop's loose fittin' clothes
I'll have a mixed drink always near at hand
Noddin' my head to the beat of a steel drum band
Watch as the sun sets from my private dock
I'll never have to punch another time clock
It will be happy hour all of the time
Now wouldn't that just be fine
Hidin' out from the world wearin' my dark tinted Ray Bans
Chillin' my life away building castles in the sands

There & Back

O where have I been
You're askin' of me
To hell & back
On the bounding Seven Seas
I've been known to blow a fuse or two
But make no mistake I always thought of you
Had my heart wrapped around a sentimental ballad
Miss your lovin' & cookin' pass me the salad
It was my fault that led me astray
Or so many of your friends will say
Departed Tuscaloosa arrived in Argentina
Found myself in a jam at a Mexican cantina
Was accused and jailed for committing a crime
Told the kangaroo court I'll pay the fine if you do my time
And you wonder where, have I been
I was tempted by an angel and sashayed into sin
Had the devil absolve me then went on my way
Damned if you do because there's always hell to pay
I've been east, I've been west
Sorry if you came up short but I tried my best
You can't always have a picnic and never expect rain
Or have a senior moment strolling down memory lane
Now I'm back never to roam
Can't promise you that I have no home
I'm like the white buffalo lost out on the range
Hunted by the Indians without their war paint, how very strange

Fox Tales

Depicted so vividly on canvas forever frozen in time
If you let me into your poem, I'll let you into mine

Sound Check

Once upon a time the music would go round and round
On black vinyl the needle found the groove producing the sound
We'd all tune in as the records played on the radio
Of Chuck Berry, Little Richard, Jerry Lee Lewis, Fats Domino
Fly me to the moon take all of my troubles away
I've got stacks of 45's old albums just waiting to play
You've got to get up in the morning with a smile on your face
Then all your cares will drift right into space
Up on the roof, under the boardwalk, over the mountain, beyond the sea
Mack the Knife, Johnny B. Goode, Stagger Lee, you and me
Robert Johnson went to the crossroads one fateful day
Then the devil went down to Georgia and Johnny fiddled him on his way
From Woody Guthrie's pasture of plenty
To Jackson Browne's running on empty
Themes and schemes
Lost love and dreams
Dale had Roy and Sonny had his Cher
Les Paul and Mary Ford an extraordinary talented pair
Give me that old time religion, a spiritual hymn
Show me, the way to San Jose take me out on a limb

Fox Tales

Buddy Holly, the Big Bopper, Richie Valens the holy trinity
Eleanor Rigby, Sgt. Pepper, Yesterday, Let It Be
And the beat goes on, light my fire
Papa's got a brand new bag I want to take you higher
Elton John, David Bowie and Billy Joel
The Righteous Brothers blue eyed soul
Janis took a piece of our heart
Jimi took Woodstock to the woodshed and blew it all apart
Country, Delta Blues, Jazz, Western Swing
Hank Williams, Muddy Waters, Thelonious Monk, Bob Wills all were king
From mono to hi fidelity stereo
Give it a listen, hey you'll never know
Music is history has significance to me
Fond memories of days gone by, that keeps me company
The ink is black the page is white
Teach your children wrong from right
Hail to the chief for he's so vain
The president needs to guard the Tomb of the Unknown Soldier
In in a hurricane
I'll buy you boots made from Spanish leather
Looks like we're in for nasty weather
In one word R E S P E C T
That is what the Wounded Warriors deserve from you and me
The time has come today
Stopped into a church I passed along the way
Slip slidin' away ole' ole' ole'
Sitting on the dock of the bay
Mama told me not to come

James R. Fox

You and I march to the beat of a different drum
So many great tunes that had the right stuff
As a skilled carpenter shapes a piece of wood
Smoothing and sanding just enough
Sundays will never be the same
Because I left the cake out in the rain
I grew up in New York City
Where the streets were tough and the girls were so pretty
Now these days, I'm out here in the sticks
Surrounded by corn fields, a cemetery, hayseed hicks
Plant the flowers while working on a farmers tan
Fill in the blanks if I have a loss for words whenever I can
Less stress these days flying the flag feeding the birds
Attend church bow my head pray and recite the holy words
And the music goes round and round
Keeps us all firmly planted to the ground

Thank you for reading.
Please review this book. Reviews help others find Absolutely Amazing Ebooks and inspires us to keep providing these marvelous tales.

If you would like to be put on our email list to receive updates on new releases, contests, and promotions, please go to AbsolutelyAmazingEbooks.com and sign up.

About the Author

James R. Fox received an Associate Liberal Arts degree from Queens Borough Community College. Now retired, he devotes his attention to writing, music, photography, traveling, and reading. Among his publications are *The Wake*, *Wisdom of Wishes*, *Christmas Eve*, and *The Map of the Carpenter*. His "Key West" was selected for inclusion in *The 2013 Robert Frost International Poetry and Haiku Contest* anthology.

His novella *Tails I Win Heads You Lose* will be published later this year.

The New Atlantian Library

NewAtlantianLibrary.com
or AbsolutelyAmazingEbooks.com
or AA-eBooks.com